THE OBSERVER'S
POCKET SERIES
.   .   .

THE OBSERVER'S BOOK
OF AIRCRAFT ✍   ✍

The Observer's Books

THE OBSERVER'S BOOK OF

AIRCRAFT

Compiled by
WILLIAM GREEN

With silhouettes by
DENNIS PUNNETT

Describing
155 AIRCRAFT
with 280 illustrations

1970 Edition

FREDERICK WARNE & CO. LTD.
FREDERICK WARNE & CO. INC.
LONDON · NEW YORK

Nineteenth Edition 1970

LIBRARY OF CONGRESS CATALOG CARD NO. 57-4425

Recommended by
THE AIR SCOUTS' DEPARTMENT
of
THE SCOUTS' ASSOCIATION

7232 0087 4
Printed in Great Britain

INTRODUCTION TO THE 1970 EDITION

With the appearance of this volume of *The Observer's Book of Aircraft*—the 19th annual edition—the 'sixties have already translated to the 'seventies and aviation has entered a new decade. Time alone can tell if the next 10 years will prove as momentous in aeronautical annals as have undoubtedly the half-score now passed, but if the first of the débutantes of the 'seventies to be found in the pages that follow are any guideline there is every reason to believe that they will.

However, at this juncture it is possibly instructive to look back and peruse the pages of the *ninth* annual edition of *The Observer's Book of Aircraft*. Perhaps surprisingly in view of the unprecedented momentum of aeronautical design and development over the past decade, it will be found that more than 16 per cent of the aircraft described and illustrated in this 1970 volume are also to be found in the edition of 10 years ago; aeroplanes which, if production longevity be taken as a yardstick, represent the true successes of the 'sixties.

The military aircraft, which include the Buccaneer, Lightning, Orion, Mirage, Skyhawk, Starfighter, Phantom II, Northrop F-5, Draken and Vigilante, were, in 1960, on the thresholds of their service careers, and their production now continues into the 'seventies. Commercial transports are fewer, being represented by only the Caravelle, Friendship and DC-8, a trio that have appeared in one or another variant in each of the last 10 successive volumes yet bid fair to remain with us for some time to come, while rotorcraft contenders in the production longevity stakes include the Iroquois, Mil Mi-6, Alouette III, Sikorsky S-61 and Chinook.

With this edition they are joined by many new aircraft, and it is interesting to speculate as to which of these will still find a place in the 1980 edition. Less crystal-gazing is demanded, however, to conjecture that this first *year* of the 'seventies will at least equal and perhaps surpass its equivalent of the last decade as a true vintage year from the aeronautical viewpoint, for at least a half-dozen exciting new commercial aircraft, such as the DC-10, L-1011 TriStar, VFW 614, Mercure, Falcon 10, and SN-600 Corvette, may be expected to commence their flight test programmes or at least be rolled out of the factories in which they are now taking shape, while the ranks of military aircraft are likely to be joined by the Grumman F-14A and NAMC C-1A.

WILLIAM GREEN

AERMACCHI M.B.326G

Country of Origin: Italy.

Type: Tandem two-seat basic trainer and light strike aircraft.

Power Plant: One Rolls-Royce Bristol Viper 20 Mk. 540 turbojet rated at 3,410 lb.s.t.

Performance: (Trainer at 8,680 lb.) Max. speed, 524 m.p.h. at 20,000 ft.; max. cruise, 495 m.p.h.; initial climb, 6,050 ft./min.; service ceil., 47,000 ft.; range (with tip tanks), 1,150 mls., (plus underwing tanks), 1,520 mls.

Weights: Basic operational (trainer), 5,920 lb.; max. loaded (trainer), 10,090 lb., (strike), 11,500 lb.

Armament: Four wing hardpoints each stressed to lift 1,000 lb. of ordnance plus two hardpoints stressed to carry 750 lb. Maximum ordnance load of 4,325 lb.

Status: M.B.326G is more powerful, dual-role version of basic M.B.326, and first of two prototypes flown on May 9, 1967. In production for *Aeronautica Militare* and for export (M.B.326GB) to Argentina, Brazil and the Congo.

Notes: First M.B.326 flown on December 10, 1957 and subsequently built with 2,500 lb. Viper 11 for *Aeronautica Militare* (100 examples), Tunisia as M.B.326B (eight examples), Ghana as M.B.326F (seven examples), Australia as M.B.326H, and South Africa as M.B.326M. Both M.B.326H and 326M licence built in respective countries, the latter as the Atlas Impala.

6

AERMACCHI M.B.326G

Dimensions: Span (over tip tanks), 35 ft. 7¼ in.; length,
34 ft. 11¼ in.; height, 12 ft. 2½ in.; wing area, 208·3 sq.
ft.

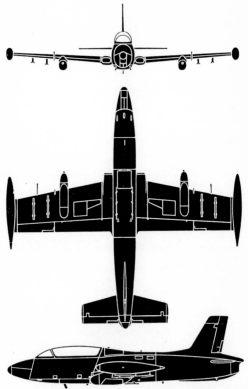

AERO L 39

Country of Origin: Czechoslovakia.
Type: Tandem two-seat basic trainer and light strike aircraft.
Power Plant: One Walter Titan (Ivchenko AI-25V) turbofan rated at 3,307 lb.s.t.
Performance: (Figures in parentheses relate to production model with 3,968 lb. Titan) Max. speed, 373 (466) m.p.h. at sea level, 444 (503) m.p.h. at 16,400 ft.; initial climb, 3,740 (5,315) ft./min.; time to 16,400 ft., 5 (2·8) min.; range at 8,598 lb., (590) mls., at 9,480 lb., (900) mls.
Weights: Normal loaded, 8,598 lb.; max. loaded, 9,480 lb.
Armament: Four wing hardpoints for up to 4,410 lb. ordnance.
Status: First of four prototypes (of which two for static tests) flown November 4, 1968. First production aircraft scheduled to be completed late 1970 or early 1971.
Notes: Designed as a successor to the L 29 Delfin, the Aero L 39 is intended primarily for use by the Warsaw Pact air forces. The production model (illustrated on opposite page) differs from the first flying prototype (illustrated above) in a number of respects, and will initially be powered by a version of the Titan rated at 3,307 lb. thrust. Subsequent production aircraft will have an uprated engine of 3,968 lb.

8

AERO L 39

Dimensions: Span (over tip tanks), 29 ft. 10⅔ in.; length, 39 ft. 10⅔ in.; height, 14 ft. 4¼ in.; wing area, 202·36 sq. ft.

ANTONOV AN-22 ANTEI (COCK)

Country of Origin: U.S.S.R.
Type: Long-range military and commercial freighter.
Power Plants: Four Kuznetsov NK-12MA turboprops each rated at 15,000 e.h.p.
Performance: Max. speed, 460 m.p.h.; max. cruise, 422 m.p.h.; cruising altitude, 26,250–32,800 ft.; range (with 99,208-lb. payload), 6,835 mls. at 373 m.p.h., (with 176,370-lb. payload), 3,107 mls. at 404 m.p.h.
Weights: Empty equipped, 251,327 lb.; max. take-off, 551,156 lb.
Accommodation: Crew of 5–6 and cabin for 28–29 passengers between freight hold and flight deck. Freight hold can accommodate three tracked carriers for single Frog or twin Ganef surface-to-surface missiles, self-propelled guns, etc.
Status: First of five prototypes flown February 27, 1965. Two prototypes delivered to Soviet Air Force and three to Aeroflot. First production aircraft (for Soviet Air Force) flown spring 1967. Production for commercial operation envisaged as 30 per year.
Notes: The An-22 was designed primarily to meet a Soviet Air Force requirement for a heavy strategic transport, and possessed the distinction of being the world's largest aircraft until the appearance of the C-5A Galaxy. By late 1968 it was known to be in service with several Sov. A.F. units. A modified version for Aeroflot actively under development will provide accommodation for 605 passengers or 383 passengers and 66,140 lb. freight, these loads being carried over 1,865 miles.

ANTONOV AN-22 ANTEI (COCK)

Dimensions: Span, 211 ft. 3½ in.; length 189 ft. 8 in.; height, 41 ft. 0 in.; wing area, 5,166·68 sq. ft.

ANTONOV AN-26

Country of Origin: U.S.S.R.

Type: Short- to medium-range military and commercial freight transport.

Power Plants: Two Ivchenko AI-24T turboprops each rated at 2,820 e.s.h.p. and one Tumansky RU-19-300 turbojet rated at 1,980 lb.s.t.

Performance: Max. speed, 335 m.p.h. at 19,685 ft.; max. cruise, 280 m.p.h. at 19,685 ft.; range (with 3,307-lb. payload and reserves), 1,553 mls., (with 11,023-lb. payload and reserves), 808 mls.; service ceil., 24,935 ft.

Weights: Empty equipped, 37,258 lb.; max. take-off, 52,911 lb.

Accommodation: Normal crew of five with folding seats for up to 38 passengers/troops along main cabin walls. Direct rear loading for freight or vehicles and provision for air-dropping over rear ramp, and manually- or electrically-operated conveyor with 9,920-lb. capacity in floor.

Status: Prototype reportedly commenced flight trials in 1968, and production for both military and commercial use believed to have commenced 1969.

Notes: Derivative of An-24RT intended for both military and civil applications, the An-26 features a completely redesigned rear fuselage of 'beavertail' type and large paradrop observation blisters below and aft of flight deck. Like An-24RT, the An-26 has an auxiliary turbojet in the starboard engine nacelle. The hold can accommodate various military vehicles, including the UAZ-469 and GAZ-69.

ANTONOV AN-26

Dimensions: Span, 95 ft. 10 in.; length, 77 ft. 2½ in.; height, 27 ft. 4 in.; wing area, 779·845 sq. ft.

BAC ONE-ELEVEN SERIES 500

Country of Origin: United Kingdom.
Type: Short- to medium-range commercial transport.
Power Plants: Two Rolls-Royce Spey 25 Mk. 512-14DW turbofans each rated at 12,460 lb.s.t.
Performance: Max. cruise, 548 m.p.h. at 21,000 ft.; long-range cruise, 472 m.p.h. at 35,000 ft.; range with max. payload (23,405 lb.) and nil reserves, 1,850 mls. at 35,000 ft.; range with max. fuel, nil reserves and zero payload, 2,885 mls.
Weights: Basic operational, 54,595 lb.; max. take-off, 98,000 lb.
Accommodation: Basic flight crew of two and high-density seating for 109 passengers. Typical mixed-class seating for 12 first-class and 79 coach-class passengers.
Status: In production with first delivery (to BEA) on August 29, 1968. Fifty-three ordered by January 1, 1970. Aerodynamic prototype flown on June 30, 1967.
Notes: By comparison with predecessors (see 1967 edition), the Series 500 features uprated engines, a 13 ft. 6 in. increase in overall length, and a redesigned wing with re-profiled leading edge, bigger tips increasing span and area by 5 ft. and 51 sq. ft. respectively, and modified flap-track fairings. With the Series 500 wing and similar uprated engines, the shorter-fuselage Series 400 becomes the Series 475 for hot and high environments. The Series 500 serves with BEA as the Super One-Eleven, other operators including British United Airways, Court and Caledonian Airways.

BAC ONE-ELEVEN SERIES 500

Dimensions: Span, 93 ft. 6 in.; length, 107 ft. 0 in.;
height, 24 ft. 6 in.; wing area, 1,031 sq. ft.

BAC LIGHTNING F. MK. 53

Country of Origin: United Kingdom.
Type: Single-seat interceptor, strike and reconnaissance fighter.
Power Plants: Two Rolls-Royce RB.146 Avon 302-C turbojets each rated at 11,100 lb.s.t. and 16,300 lb.s.t. with afterburning.
Performance: (Estimated) Max. speed, 1,500 m.p.h. at 40,000 ft. (Mach 2·27); long-range cruise, 595 m.p.h. at 36,000–40,000 ft.; initial climb, 50,000 ft./min.; time to 40,000 ft. 2·5 min.
Weights: Estimated max. loaded, 50,000 lb.
Armament: Interchangeable packs containing the equipment for two Red Top or Firestreak AAMs, or 44 2-in. rockets, plus two 30-mm. Aden cannon with 120 r.p.g. in ventral pack, plus two 1,000-lb. bombs or two MATRA 155 launchers for 18 SNEB 68-mm. rockets.
Status: First F. Mk. 53 flown November 1, 1966, and first delivery (Royal Saudi A.F.) on December 4, 1967. In production for Saudi Arabia and Kuwait.
Notes: Multi-mission export version of F. Mk. 6 interceptor for R.A.F. (see 1968 edition). Provision for two 260 Imp. gal. overwing ferry tanks. Developed version (illustrated opposite) can carry twin MATRA 155 launchers on each underwing pylon, plus twin MATRA launchers (each with 18 SNE Brockets and 50 Imp. gal. fuel) on overwing pylons, giving total of 144 68-mm. rockets. Reconnaissance packs may be fitted.

16

BAC LIGHTNING F. MK. 53

Dimensions: Span, 34 ft. 10 in.; length (including probe), 55 ft. 3 in.; height, 19 ft. 7 in.; approximate wing area, 460 sq. ft.

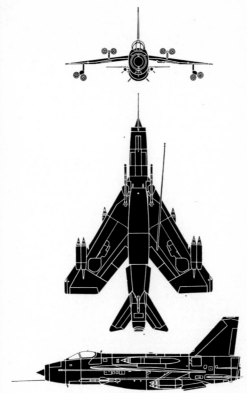

BAC 167 STRIKEMASTER

Country of Origin: United Kingdom.

Type: Side-by-side two-seat basic trainer and light attack and counter-insurgency aircraft.

Power Plant: One Rolls-Royce Bristol Viper 535 (20-F.20) turbojet rated at 3,410 lb.s.t.

Performance: Max. speed, 481 m.p.h. at 20,000 ft.; initial climb (at 10,823 lb.), 3,200 ft./min.; time to 20,000 ft. (at 10,823 lb.), 9 min.; range (for navigational training at 8,940 lb. with 10% reserves), 985 mls.; tactical radius (with four MATRA rocket pods, 48 Imp. gal. wingtip tank and 7 min. over target), 253 mls., (with two MATRA pods, wingtip tanks, two 75 Imp. gal. underwing tanks), 449 mls., (with wingtip and four 75 Imp. gal. underwing tanks), 628 mls.

Weights: Empty, 5,850 lb.; loaded (pilot training), 8,050 lb., (navigational training with wingtip tanks), 8,940 lb., (two guns, four MATRA pods and tip tanks), 10,823 lb.; max. loaded, 11,500 lb.

Armament: Two 7·62-mm. F.N. machine guns with 590 r.p.g., plus four MATRA 155 pods each with 18 SNEB 68-mm. rockets, four pods each with 36 2-in. rockets, 32 80-mm. rockets, or four 500-lb. bombs.

Status: First flown October 26, 1967. In production. First deliveries late 1968.

Notes: The Strikemaster is essentially similar to the BAC 145 Jet Provost T.5 (see 1966 edition) but employs a more powerful engine. Strikemasters are being delivered to the Saudi, Sudanese, Muscat and Oman, Kuwaiti and Singapore air arms.

18

BAC 167 STRIKEMASTER

Dimensions: Span, 35 ft. 4 in., (over tip tanks), 36 ft. 11 in.; length, 33 ft. 7½ in.; height, 10 ft. 2 in.; wing area, 213·7 sq. ft.

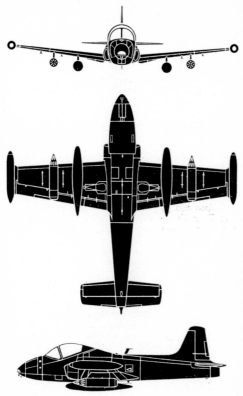

BAC SUPER VC10

Country of Origin: United Kingdom.

Type: Long-range commercial transport.

Power Plants: Four Rolls-Royce Conway RCo 43 turbofans each rated at 22,500 lb.s.t.

Performance: Max. cruise, 581 m.p.h. at 31,000 ft.; econ. cruise, 550 m.p.h. at 38,000 ft.; initial climb, 2,300 ft./min.; range with max. fuel (25,452-lb. payload and no reserves), 7,128 mls.; range with max. payload (59,620 lb.), 4,720 mls.

Weights: Basic operational, 155,380 lb.; max. take-off, 335,000 lb.

Accommodation: Basic flight crew of five and 163–174 economy-class passengers or a mixed payload such as 32 first-class and 99 economy-class passengers.

Status: First Super VC10 (Model 1151 for BOAC) flown for first time on May 7, 1964. Entered service on April 1, 1965 (with BOAC). Production completed 1969 with 54 (of all versions) delivered.

Notes: The Super VC10 is a stretched version of the basic VC10 with a 13-ft. increase in fuselage length, repositioned rear cabin door and rear freight hold door, a fuel tank in the fin and uprated turbofans. The basic VC10 can accommodate 135–151 economy-class passengers, and has been delivered to BOAC (Model 1101), Ghana Airways (Model 1102), and British United Airways (Model 1103). Fourteen for R.A.F. Air Support Command (Model 1106) have similar engines and fin tank to Super VC10 and are operated by No. 10 Sqdn. as the VC10 C. Mk. 1 (see 1969 edition). The Super VC10 is operated by BOAC (Model 1151) and East African Airways (Model 1154).

BAC SUPER VC10

Dimensions: Span, 146 ft. 2 in.; length, 105 ft. 0 in.;
height, 39 ft. 6 in.; wing area, 2,932 sq. ft.

BAC/BREGUET JAGUAR

Countries of Origin: United Kingdom and France.

Type: Single-seat tactical strike fighter (A and S) and two-seat advanced trainer (B and E).

Power Plants: Two Rolls-Royce-Turboméca RB. 172/T-260 Adour turbofans each rated at 4,600 lb.s.t. and 6,900 lb.s.t. with afterburning.

Performance: (Jaguar A) Max. speed, 820 m.p.h. at 1,000 ft. (Mach 1·1), 1,130 m.p.h. at 33,000 ft. (Mach 1·7), 925 m.p.h. at 42,000 ft. (Mach 1·4); tactical radius on internal fuel with typical military load (lo-lo-lo mission profile), 400 mls., (hi-lo-hi), 775 mls.; maximum ferry range, 2,800 mls.

Weights: Approx. normal loaded, 22,050 lb.; max. overload, 30,865 lb.

Armament: Two 30-mm. cannon and max. external ordnance load of up to 10,000 lb. on one fuselage and four underwing pylons.

Status: First of eight prototypes flown September 8, 1968. First of 200 ordered for *Armée de l'Air* scheduled to enter service 1971 with first of similar quantity ordered for R.A.F. entering service in 1972.

Notes: Five versions under simultaneous development in Anglo-French programme: A (*Appui Tactique*) and E (*Ecole de Combat*) respectively single-seat tactical support and two-seat training versions for the *Armée de l'Air*, M (*Marine*) single-seat shipboard version for the *Aéronavale*, and the S and B which are respectively single-seat strike and two-seat training versions for the R.A.F. The first British-assembled aircraft (illustrated), the Jaguar S.06, was flown for first time on October 12, 1969.

22

BAC/BREGUET JAGUAR

Dimensions: Span, 27 ft. 10¼ in.; length, 50 ft. 11 in.; height, 15 ft. 2⅔ in.; wing area, 258·33 sq. ft.

BAC/SUD-AVIATION CONCORDE

Countries of Origin: United Kingdom and France.
Type: Long-haul supersonic commercial transport.
Power Plants: Four Rolls-Royce Bristol/SNECMA
Olympus 593 Stage O turbojets each rated at 32,825
lb.s.t. and 37,420 lb.s.t. with afterburning.
Performance: (Estimated) Range cruise, 1,350–1,385
m.p.h. (Mach 2·05–2·1) at 55,000–62,000 ft.; range
with max. fuel, nil reserves and 19,800-lb. payload,
5,595 mls.; range with max. payload (nominal 28,000
lb.) and nil reserves, 5,215 mls. at 58,000 ft. (Mach 2·1);
range with max. payload and FAR reserves, 4,020 mls.
Weights: Basic operational, 169,000 lb.; max. take-off
385,000 lb.
Accommodation: Maximum high-density seating for
144 passengers and typical mixed-class arrangement
for 12 first-class and 102 coach-class passengers.
Status: First and second prototypes flown on March
2, 1969 (at Toulouse) and April 9, 1969 (at Filton).
First (at Filton) and second (at Toulouse) pre-production aircraft scheduled to fly by early 1971, with first
three production aircraft commencing testing in 1972.
Notes: Changes to be introduced by pre-production
aircraft (described above) will include increase in
overall length to 193 ft., a stepped fuselage nose and
redesigned visor, and wider-chord wingtips. Air-
worthiness certification is scheduled for 1973, and
Stage 1 engines with non-augmented rating of 35,080
lb.s.t. will be introduced after two years of operation.
First supersonic flight took place on October 1, 1969.

BAC/SUD-AVIATION CONCORDE

Dimensions: (Prototypes) Span, 83 ft. 10 in.; length, 184 ft. 2 in.; height, 38 ft. 0 in.; wing area, 3,856 sq. ft.

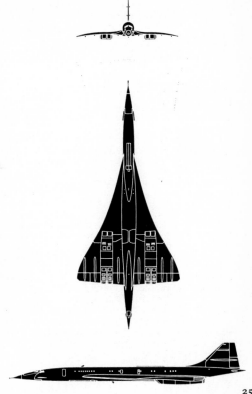

BEAGLE B.121 PUP

Country of Origin: United Kingdom.
Type: (Pup-100) Two- or (Pup-150) two/three-seat light cabin monoplane.
Power Plant: One (Pup-100) Rolls Royce Continental O-200A or (Pup-150) Lycoming O-320-A2B four-cylinder horizontally-opposed engine rated at 100 h.p. and 150 h.p. respectively.
Performance: (Specification relates to Pup-100 with figures in parentheses applying to the Pup-150) Max. speed, 127 (138) m.p.h. at sea level; cruise at 75% power, 118 (131) m.p.h. at 7,000 (7,500) ft.; range with 24 Imp. gal., 569 (440) mls. at 4,000 (10,000) ft., with 34 Imp. gal., (633) mls.; initial climb rate, 575 (800) ft./min.; service ceil., 11,200 (14,700) ft.
Weights: Empty, 1,063 (1,151) lb.; max. take-off, 1,600 (1,925) lb.
Accommodation: Side-by-side seats for two persons with baggage space for 85 (120) lb. An optional third seat is available for the Pup-150.
Status: In production, with 100th delivered on September 23, 1969, and a further 120 scheduled for delivery by April 1970 when output is expected to attain two per day. Prototype Pup-100 flown April 8, 1967 and prototype Pup-150 on October 4, 1967.
Notes: The Pup-150 is illustrated, and the Pup-180 is a proposed four-seater with a 180 h.p. Lycoming O-360-A engine.

BEAGLE B.121 PUP

Dimensions: Span, 31 ft. 0 in.; length, 22 ft. 11 in. (23 ft. 2 in.); height, 7 ft. 6¼ in.; wing area, 120 sq. ft.

BEAGLE B.125 BULLDOG

Country of Origin: United Kingdom.
Type: Side-by-side two-seat military primary trainer.
Power Plant: One Lycoming IO-360-A1C four-cylinder horizontally-opposed engine rated at 200 h.p.
Performance: Max. speed, 162 m.p.h. at sea level; max. cruise, 153 m.p.h. at 5,000 ft.; econ. cruise (at 55% power), 148 m.p.h. at 15,000 ft.; initial climb, 1,100 ft./min.; range with max. fuel and max. payload (at 55% power at 4,000 ft.), 628 mls.
Weights: Empty, 1,398 lb.; max. loaded, 2,350 lb.
Status: Prototype flown on May 19, 1969 with production deliveries scheduled to commence mid-1970.
Notes: The Bulldog is a derivative of the B.121 Pup (see pages 26–27) intended for military primary training, and orders placed for the Bulldog during 1969 include 58 (plus an option of a further 45) for the Swedish Air Force, eight for the Zambian Air Force, and five for the Kenya Air Force. Apart from a more powerful engine and structural strengthening, the Bulldog differs from the Pup in having a blown, aft-sliding jettisonable cockpit canopy, trimmable rudder and elevators, increased fuel capacity, and larger wheels. In addition the overall wing span has been increased. The Bulldog is a potential successor to the Chipmunk as an R.A.F. Training Command *ab initio* trainer.

BEAGLE B.125 BULLDOG

Dimensions: Span, 33 ft. 0 in.; length, 23 ft. 2½ in.; height, 7 ft. 5¾ in.; wing area, 128·5 sq. ft.

BEECHCRAFT MODEL 60 DUKE

Country of Origin: U.S.A.

Type: Four-to-six-seat light cabin monoplane.

Power Plants: Two Lycoming TIO-541-E1A4 six-cylinder horizontally-opposed engines each rated at 380 h.p.

Performance: Max. speed, 286 m.p.h. at 23,000 ft.; cruise at 75% power, 246 m.p.h. at 15,000 ft.; 258 m.p.h. at 20,000 ft., 271 m.p.h. at 25,000 ft., at 65% power, 232 m.p.h. at 15,000 ft., 243 m.p.h. at 20,000 ft., 255 m.p.h. at 25,000 ft.; initial climb, 1,615 ft./min.; service ceil., 31,300 ft.; range (with max. optional fuel and 45 min. reserves), 973 mls. at 75% power at 25,000 ft., 1,073 mls. at 65% power at 25,000 ft., 1,175 mls. at 45% power at 25,000 ft.

Weights: Empty equipped, 4,100 lb.; max. take-off, 6,725 lb.

Accommodation: Standard model has four individual seats in pairs with central aisle, but additional fifth and sixth seats are optional.

Status: Prototype flown December 29, 1966 with production deliveries commencing in July 1968, 31 being delivered during the course of that year and deliveries averaging eight per month during 1969.

Notes: The Duke is the fastest and one of the cheapest pressurised aircraft in its category, and is the smallest aircraft to be built with side entry door and central aisle between the seats.

30

BEECHCRAFT MODEL 60 DUKE

Dimensions: Span, 39 ft. 4 in.; length, 34 ft. 0 in.; height, 12 ft. 4 in.; wing area, 213 sq. ft.

BEECHCRAFT MODEL 99A

Country of Origin: U.S.A.
Type: Light commercial feederliner.
Power Plants: Two Pratt & Whitney PT6A-27 turbo-props each rated at 652 e.s.h.p.
Performance: Max. cruise, 273 m.p.h. at 3,000 ft., 284 m.p.h. at 10,000 ft.; econ. cruise, 279 m.p.h. at 8,000 ft.; max. range cruise, 216 m.p.h. at 8,000 ft.; initial climb, 1,700 ft./min.; service ceil., 26,200 ft.; range, 887 mls. at 279 m.p.h. at 8,000 ft., 1,048 mls. at 216 m.p.h. at 8,000 ft.
Weights: Empty equipped (standard 15-seater), 5,533 lb.; max. take-off, 10,400 lb.
Accommodation: Normal flight crew of two and 15 passengers in individual seats on each side of central aisle. Optional 8-seat business executive transport arrangement. An 800-lb. capacity ventral cargo pod may be fitted.
Status: Prototype Model 99 first flown July 1966, and first production delivery effected on May 2, 1968, 62 being delivered by end of year. Thirty-sixth production Model 99 converted as prototype Model 99A, deliveries of which commenced 1969.
Notes: A hybrid employing the wings of the Queen Air and the engines and nacelles of the King Air (see pages 34–35), with sub-systems from both, the Model 99 has 579 e.s.h.p. PT6A-20s but is otherwise similar to the Model 99A. A pressurised version for 1971 service is currently under study.

32

BEECHCRAFT MODEL 99A

Dimensions: Span, 45 ft. 10½ in.; length, 44 ft. 6¾ in.; height, 14 ft. 4⅓ in.; wing area, 279·7 sq. ft.

BEECHCRAFT MODEL A97 KING AIR 100

Country of Origin: U.S.A.
Type: Light commercial feederliner and business executive transport.
Power Plants: Two Pratt & Whitney PT6A-28 turbo-props each rated at 680 s.h.p.
Performance: Max. cruise, 287 m.p.h. at 12,000 ft., 274 m.p.h. at 21,000 ft.; initial climb, 2,200 ft./min.; service ceil., 25,900 ft.; max. range (including normal allowances and 45 min. reserves), 1,245 mls. at 21,000 ft.
Weights: Empty equipped, 6,405 lb.; max. take-off, 10,600 lb.
Accommodation: Normal flight crew of two and seating for six passengers in standard business executive layout. Variety of alternative cabin configurations including 15-seat feederliner version.
Status: King Air 100 initially flown in spring of 1969 with first production delivery in September of that year when initial production rate was planned at nine per month for 1970.
Notes: Third generation development of King Air series with lengthened fuselage, enlarged vertical tail, dual-wheel main undercarriage members, and more powerful engines. Original Model 90 King Air flown January 20, 1964 with PT6A-6 turboprops. Succeeded in 1966 by A90 with PT6A-20s and B90 with increased wing span (50 ft. 3 in.).

BEECHCRAFT MODEL A97 KING AIR 100

Dimensions: Span, 45 ft. 10½ in.; length, 39 ft. 11½ in.; height, 15 ft. 4¾ in.; wing area, 277·06 sq. ft.

BERIEV BE-12 (MAIL)

Country of Origin: U.S.S.R.
Type: Maritime patrol and reconnaissance amphibian.
Power Plants: Two Ivchenko AI-20D turboprops each rated at 4,190 s.h.p.
Performance: (Estimated) Max. speed, 380 m.p.h.; normal patrol speed, 200–250 m.p.h. at 5,000 ft.; initial climb 3,000 ft./min.; service ceiling, 37,000 ft.; max. range, 2,500 mls.
Weights: Approx. loaded, 60,000–65,000 lb.
Status: In production and in service.
Notes: Reportedly flown in prototype form in 1960, the Be-12 is the successor to the piston-engined Be-6 with Soviet maritime patrol units, and follows closely the basic configuration of its predecessor. During 1964, the Be-12 established six officially-recognised international altitude records in the FAI class C.3 Group II for turboprop-powered amphibians. These records included an altitude of 39,977 ft. without payload, an altitude of 37,290 ft. with payloads of 2,205 and 4,409 lb., an altitude of 30,682 ft. with a 22,046-lb. payload, and a maximum payload of 22,266 lb. lifted to an altitude of 6,560 ft. On April 24, 1968, a Be-12 established a C.3 Group II 310·6-mile closed-circuit speed record of 343 m.p.h., and two days later established a similar record in C.2 Group II of 351 m.p.h. The largest amphibian flying boat currently in service, the Be-12 is of conventional appearance with a magnetic anomaly detection extension protuding from the rear fuselage, a glazed observation position in the nose, and a fully retractable undercarriage.

BERIEV BE-12 (MAIL)

Estimated Dimensions: Span, 108 ft. 0 in.; length, 96 ft. 0 in.; height, 23 ft. 0 in.; wing area, 1,030 sq. ft.

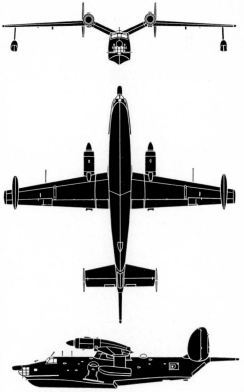

BERIEV BE-30 (CUFF)

Country of Origin: U.S.S.R.

Type: Light commercial feederliner.

Power Plants: Two TVD-10 turboprops each rated at 970 e.s.h.p.

Performance: Max. speed, 304 m.p.h.; max. cruise, 286 m.p.h. at 6,500 ft.; range (with 1,984-lb. payload, normal allowances and 30 min. reserves), 620 mls at 236 m.p.h., (with 2,755-lb. payload), 373 mls.; max. range (with 1,543-lb. payload), 810 mls.

Weights: Empty equipped, 7,937 lb.; max. take-off, 12,919 lb.

Accommodation: Normal flight crew of two and seats for 14–16 passengers in standard arrangement. Alternative high-density arrangement (Be-30A) for 21–23 passengers.

Status: First prototype flown (with ASh-21 piston engines) on March 3, 1967, followed by definitive series prototype on July 18, 1968. First production deliveries (to Aeroflot) mid-1969.

Notes: Designed specifically for use by Aeroflot on local service routes and operating from short, grass strips, the Be-30 is also being developed for the light freighter, aerial survey and ambulance roles. The original project envisaged the interconnection of the two turboprops so that one power plant would drive both airscrews in the event of the other failing but there is no evidence that this feature has been retained.

BERIEV BE-30 (CUFF)

Dimensions: Span, 55 ft. 9¼ in.; length, 50 ft. 10¼ in.; height, 18 ft. 3¼ in.; wing area, 344·445 sq. ft.

BOEING MODEL 727-200

Country of Origin: U.S.A.

Type: Short- and medium-range commercial transport.

Power Plants: Three Pratt & Whitney JT8D-9 turbofans each rated at 14,500 lb.s.t.

Performance: Max. speed (at 169,000 lb.), 630 m.p.h. at 22,000 ft.; max. cruise, 592 m.p.h. at 18,000 ft.; econ. cruise, 553 m.p.h. at 30,000 ft.; range (with max. payload—42,275 lb.), 1,130 mls., (max. fuel and 25,000-lb. payload), 2,300 mls.

Weights: Operational empty, 93,725 lb.; max. take-off, 169,000 lb.

Accommodation: Alternative arrangements available for 179 passengers in high-density configuration, 180 tourist-class passengers, 163 tourist-class passengers, or 14 first-class and 130 tourist-class passengers.

Status: In production. First Model 727-200 flown July 27, 1967, obtaining FAA certification four months later, on November 30, and first delivery (to Northeast) was effected December 11, 1967. The 500th Model 727 (a 727-200 for National) was delivered on December 26, 1967, and approximately 780 Model 727s had been delivered by the beginning of 1970.

Notes: The Model 727-200 is a "stretched" development of the basic Model 727-100 (see 1966 edition) to meet the requirements of the high-density commuter-type market and differs primarily in having two 10-ft. fuselage sections added, one forward and the other aft of the wing. The Models 727-100C and -100QC are convertible cargo-passenger versions of the short-body Model 727.

BOEING MODEL 727-200

Dimensions: Span, 108 ft. 0 in.; length, 153 ft. 2 in.; height, 34 ft. 0 in.; wing area, 1,700 sq. ft.

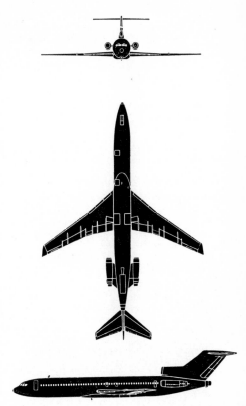

BOEING MODEL 737-200

Country of Origin: U.S.A.

Type: Short-haul commercial transport.

Power Plants: Two Pratt & Whitney JT8D-9 turbo-fans each rated at 14,500 lb.s.t.

Performance: Max. cruise, 573 m.p.h. at 26,000 ft.; typical cruise, 506 m.p.h. at 30,000 ft.; range (with max. payload—31,931 lb.), 2,080 mls.; initial climb, 3,200 ft./min.

Weights: Operational empty, 59,225 lb.; max. take-off, 111,000 lb.

Accommodation: Flight crew of two and alternative arrangements for 88 passengers in five-abreast seating, 91 passengers in mixed-class (28 passengers four abreast and 63 passengers six abreast) seating, or 113 passengers in six-abreast seating.

Status: In production. First Model 737-100 flown on April 9, 1967, followed by the first Model 737-200 on August 8, 1967. First delivery of 737-100 (to Lufthansa) effected in December 1967, and first delivery of 737-200 (to United Airlines) December 29, 1967. Approximately 230 Model 737s delivered by beginning of 1970 when orders exceeded 260.

Notes: A "long-body" derivative of the Model 737-100, the Model 737-200 introduced a 6-ft. increase in overall fuselage length, and is also offered in 737-200C and 737-200QC convertible passenger/freighter versions. New thrust reversers and a series of drag reduction modifications introduced with 135th aircraft delivered March 1969.

BOEING MODEL 737-200

Dimensions: Span, 93 ft. 0 in.; length, 100 ft. 0 in.; height, 37 ft. 0 in.; wing area, 980 sq. ft.

BOEING MODEL 747

Country of Origin: U.S.A.
Type: Long-haul large-capacity commercial transport.
Power Plants: Four Pratt & Whitney JT9D-3 turbofans each rated at 43,500 lb.s.t.
Performance: Max. cruise, 625 m.p.h. at 37,000 ft.; long-range cruise, 590 m.p.h. at 35,000 ft.; range (with normal reserves and 123,000-lb. payload), 4,600 mls., (max. fuel and 40,000-lb. payload), 7080 mls.; initial climb, 2,000 ft./min.; service ceil., 40,000 ft.
Weights: Operational empty, 353,398 lb.; max. take-off, 710,000 lb.
Accommodation: Flight crew of three–five and maximum of 490 passengers in 10-abreast seating. Various alternative arrangements for 58 first-class and 308 or 336 economy-class passengers.
Status: First Model 747 flown on February 9, 1969, with first deliveries (to Pan American) scheduled for late same year. Total of 188 ordered by 29 operators by end of 1969.
Notes: Several versions of Model 747 currently under development, including the 747B for 1971 delivery. This will have operational empty and maximum take-off weights of 364,102 and 775,000 lb. respectively, and 45,000 lb.s.t. JT9D-3W engines. From January 1972, the 747B will have the 47,000 lb.s.t. JT9D-7W, and convertible passenger/freight and all-cargo versions will be the 747B-C and 747B-F. Service introduction delayed until early 1970 as a result of an engine mounting problem.

BOEING MODEL 747

Dimensions: Span, 195 ft. 8 in.; length, 231 ft. 4 in.; height, 63 ft. 5 in.; wing area, 5,685 sq. ft.

BREGUET 1150 ATLANTIC

Country of Origin: France.
Type: Long-range maritime patrol aircraft.
Power Plants: Two Hispano-Suiza-built Rolls-Royce
Tyne R.Ty.20 Mk. 21 turboprops each rated at 6,105
e.h.p.
Performance: Max. speed, 363 m.p.h. at 19,685 ft.;
max. cruise, 342 m.p.h. at 26,250 ft.; long-range cruise,
(at 95,900 lb.), 311 m.p.h. at 26,250 ft.; max. endurance
cruise, 199 m.p.h. below 1,000 ft.; loiter endurance (to
and from patrol area at 311 m.p.h.), 12 hr. at 195 m.p.h.
at range of 620 mls.; ferry range (standard max. internal
fuel), 4,150 mls.; climb, 2,450 ft./min.; service ceil.,
32,800 ft.; max. endurance, 18 hr.
Weight: Normal loaded, 95,900 lb.
Armament: Internal weapons bay accommodates Mk.
43 Brush or L.K.4 homing torpedoes, all N.A.T.O.
standard bombs, or 386-lb. U.S. or French depth
charges.
Accommodation: Crew of twelve, seven of these being
accommodated in the central operations compartment.
Status: In production. First of three prototypes flown
on October 21, 1961. First production aircraft flown
on July 19, 1965. Total orders for 87 aircraft for
France (40), Germany (20), Netherlands (9), and Italy
(18).
Notes: Manufactured by consortium of French,
German, Belgian and Dutch companies. Atlantic
entered service in 1966 with Federal Germany's
Marinefliegergeschwader 3 and France's *Flottille* 21F.
46

BREGUET 1150 ATLANTIC

Dimensions: Span, 119 ft. 1¼ in.; length, 104 ft. 1½ in.; height, 37 ft. 1¾ in.; wing area, 1,291·67 sq. ft.

BRITTEN-NORMAN BN-2A ISLANDER

Country of Origin: United Kingdom.

Type: Light utility transport.

Power Plants: Two Lycoming O-540-E4C5 six-cylinder horizontally-opposed engines each rated at 260 h.p.

Performance: Max. speed, 168 m.p.h. at sea level; max. cruise (75% power), 157 m.p.h. at 6,500 ft.; econ. cruise (67% power), 155 m.p.h. at 9,500 ft.; range at 59% power (max. fuel), 810 mls., (max. payload), 110 mls.; initial climb, 1,150 ft./min.; service ceil., 16,200 ft.

Weights: Empty equipped, 3,500 lb.; max. take-off, 5,995 lb.

Accommodation: Flight crew of one or two, and up to 10 passengers on bench-type seats, or two casualty stretchers and two attendants for ambulance role.

Status: Prototype flown June 12, 1965 with first production aircraft following on August 20, 1966. The 100th BN-2 was rolled out on July 24, 1969 when production rate was 12 per month. Assembly from British-manufactured components undertaken by URMA in Rumania, first Rumanian-assembled aircraft flying August 11, 1969.

Notes: All BN-2As delivered since June 1, 1969 are Series 2 embodying various improvements.

48

BRITTEN-NORMAN BN-2A ISLANDER

Dimensions: Span, 49 ft. 0 in.; length, 35 ft. 7¾ in.; height, 13 ft. 8 in.; wing area, 325 sq. ft.

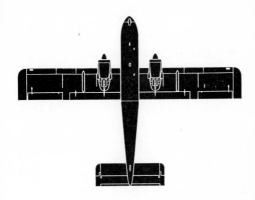

BRITTEN-NORMAN BN-3 NYMPH

Country of Origin: United Kingdom.
Type: Light cabin monoplane.
Power Plant: (Nymph 115) One Lycoming O-235-C1B four-cylinder horizontally-opposed engine rated at 115 h.p.
Performance: (Specification relates to Nymph 115 with figures in parentheses applying to the Nymph 160) Max. speed, 117 (135) m.p.h. at sea level; max. cruise at 75% power at 7,000 ft., 113 (130) m.p.h.; max. fuel range, 600 (520) mls.; initial climb, 600 (700) ft./min.; service ceil., 11,200 (12,000) ft.
Weights: Empty, 1,140 (1,250) lb.; max. take-off, 1,925 (2,350) lb.
Accommodation: Four persons in two pairs of side-by-side individual seats.
Status: Prototype (Nymph 115) flown on May 17, 1969. To be supplied by Britten-Norman in kit form for licence assembly by approved maintenance and repair organisations. First deliveries scheduled to begin September 1970.
Notes: Proposed variants include Nymph 130 (130 h.p. Continental O-240) and 160 (160 h.p. Lycoming O-320).

BRITTEN-NORMAN BN-3 NYMPH

Dimensions: Span, 39 ft. 3⅞ in.; length, 23 ft. 7¾ in.;
height, 9 ft. 6 in.; wing area, 169 sq. ft.

CANADAIR CX-84 (CL-84-1)

Country of Origin: Canada.
Type: Tilt-wing V/STOL utility aircraft.
Power Plants: Two Lycoming LTC1K-4 Cturboprops each rated at 1,500 s.h.p.
Performance: Max. speed (at 12,600 lb.), 321 m.p.h.; max. cruise (at 12,600 lb.), 309 m.p.h., (at 14,500 lb.), 301 m.p.h.; range with max. standard fuel, two min. allowances and 10% reserve (VTOL), 421 mls. (STOL) 410 mls., (VTOL with 2,315-lb. payload), 340 mls., (STOL with 4,215-lb. payload), 322 mls.
Weights: Empty, 8,437 lb.; max. take-off (VTOL), 12,600 lb., (STOL), 14,500 lb.
Accommodation: Flight crew of two and maximum of 12 passengers on inward-facing troop seats.
Status: First of three CL-84-1 prototypes scheduled to commence test programme at beginning of 1970 with second and third aircraft following by mid-1970.
Notes: The CL-84-1 tilt-wing vertical- and short-take-off-and-landing (V/STOL) has been produced for evaluation by the Canadian Armed Forces in the rescue, reconnaissance and surveillance, tactical armed support, helicopter escort and other roles. The original CL-84, which crashed in September 1967 after 305 flights, differed primarily in having 1,400 s.h.p. LTC1K-4A engines, and CL-84-1C is proposed production version with 1,800 h.p. LTC1S-2A engines.
52

CANADAIR CX-84 (CL-84-1)

Dimensions: Span, 33 ft. 4 in., (over airscrew tips), 34 ft. 8 in.; length, 47 ft. 3½ in.; height (wing tilted 90°), 17 ft. 1½ in.; wing area, 233·3 sq. ft.

CANADAIR CL-215

Country of Origin: Canada.
Type: Multi-purpose utility amphibian.
Power Plants: Two Pratt & Whitney R-2800-83AM2 radial air-cooled engines each rated at 2,100 h.p.
Performance: Max. speed, 221 m.p.h.; max. cruise, 190 m.p.h. at 8,000 ft.; range (with 7,800-lb. payload), 350 mls., (with 3,200-lb. payload), 1,250 mls.; initial climb (at 36,000 lb.), 950 ft./min.
Weights: Empty, 25,000 lb.; max. take-off (utility), 36,000 lb., (water bomber), 43,500 lb.
Accommodation: Flight crew of two and (utility) 19 passengers on canvas folding seats in main cabin, or (water bomber) two 600 Imp. gal. water tanks.
Status: First of two prototypes flown October 23, 1967 followed by first production aircraft in September 1968. First production deliveries 1969.
Notes: Development of the CL-215 was initiated and partly funded by the government of the Province of Quebec for the water-bombing of forest fires, 20 aircraft being ordered for use by the Quebec Forestry Department. Ten CL-215s have also been purchased for similar tasks by France's *Protection Civile,* and one has been leased by the Servicios Agricolas Aereos S.A. for operations in Spain. A proposed growth version is to be powered by R-2800-CB-17 engines rated at 2,200 h.p. dry and 2,500 h.p. with water injection.

54

CANADAIR CL-215

Dimensions: Span, 93 ft. 10 in.; length, 63 ft. 6½ in.;
height, 29 ft. 3 in.; wing area, 1,080 sq. ft.

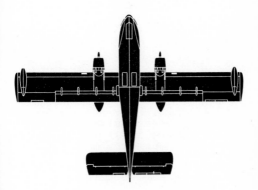

CESSNA MODEL 207 SKYWAGON

Country of Origin: U.S.A.

Type: Light utility aircraft.

Power Plant: One Continental IO-520-F six-cylinder horizontally-opposed engine rated at 300 h.p.

Performance: (At 3,800 lb.) Max. speed, 168 m.p.h. at sea level; cruise at 75% power, 158 m.p.h. at 6,500 ft., 156 m.p.h. at 8,000 ft., 152 m.p.h. at 10,000 ft.; econ. cruise, 131 m.p.h. at 10,000 ft.; range, 585 mls. at 158 m.p.h. at 6,500 ft., 695 mls. at 131 m.p.h. at 10,000 ft.; initial climb, 810 ft./min.; service ceil., 13,300 ft.

Weights: Empty (one seat only), 1,858 lb.; max. take-off 3,800 lb.

Accommodation: Single seat for pilot standard with optional individual seats for up to six passengers arranged in three pairs, two abreast.

Status: Prototype flown May 11, 1968, first production example following on January 3, 1969.

Notes: The Model 207 is essentially a stretched development of the Model U206C Super Skywagon, affording improved load-carrying ability while retaining the operating economy of its predecessor. In addition to a lengthened fuselage, the Model 207 features a separate baggage compartment forward of the cabin, and a door for the co-pilot or passenger on the starboard side at the front of the cabin. A variant of the basic aircraft is the Turbo-Skywagon with a 300 h.p. Continental TSIO-520-G turbo-supercharged engine. Production deliveries of both models commenced spring 1969.

CESSNA MODEL 207 SKYWAGON

Dimensions: Span, 36 ft. 7 in.; length, 31 ft. 9 in.;
height, 9 ft. 5 in.; wing area, 175·5 sq. ft.

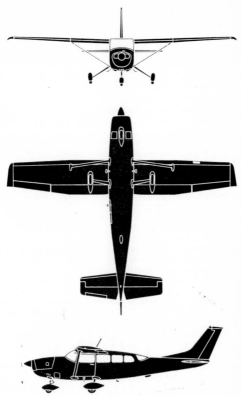

CESSNA MODEL 348 (O-2T)

Country of Origin: U.S.A.

Type: Forward air control aircraft.

Power Plants: Two Allison 250-B15 turboprops each rated at 317 s.h.p.

Performance: Max. speed, 211 m.p.h.; max. cruise (75% power), 200 m.p.h.; loiter speed, 99 m.p.h.; initial climb, 2,160 ft./min.; service ceil., 31,300 ft.

Weights: (O-2TT) Empty, 3,220 lb.; normal loaded, 5,000 lb.; max. take-off, 5,750 lb.

Accommodation: The O-2T has side-by-side seating for the two crew members, but the definitive (O-2TT) is intended to provide tandem seating for the two crew.

Armament: Four underwing armament stations each capable of lifting 350 lb.

Status: Prototype Model 348 (O-2T) flown autumn 1969. Proposed definitive production version (O-2TT) can be delivered 16 months after receipt of contract, a production rate of 21 per month being attained five months later.

Notes: The Model 348 is a conversion of the piston-engined O-2 (see 1968 edition) forward air control and psychological warfare aircraft which, in turn, is an adaptation of the commercial Model 337C Super Skymaster four–six seat cabin monoplane. A total of 377 O-2As and Bs were delivered by November 1969 for use by the U.S.A.F., and the proposed O-2TT differs from the prototype illustrated in having a lengthened fuselage with tandem seating and a longer-span wing.

CESSNA MODEL 348 (O-2T)

Dimensions: (O-2TT in parentheses) Span, 38 ft. 0 in. (43 ft. 0 in.); length, 29 ft. 9 in. (32 ft. 3½ in.); height, 9 ft. 4 in. (10 ft. 1⅛ in.); wing area, 201 (220) sq. ft.

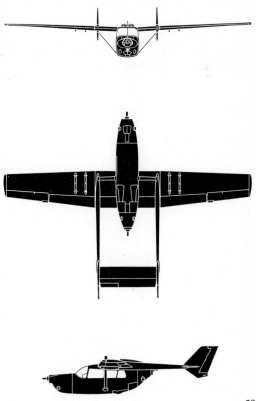

CESSNA MODEL 402-A

Country of Origin: U.S.A.

Type: Light feederliner and utility transport.

Power Plants: Two Continental TSIO-520-E six-cylinder horizontally-opposed engines each rated at 300 h.p.

Performance: (At 6,300 lb.) Max. speed, 228 m.p.h. at sea level, 261 m.p.h. at 16,000 ft.; max. cruise (75% power), 218 m.p.h. at 10,000 ft., 240 m.p.h. at 20,000 ft.; range cruise, 172 m.p.h. at 10,000 ft., 215 m.p.h. at 25,000 ft.; range (standard fuel), 660 mls. at 216 m.p.h. at 10,000 ft. at 75% power, 694 mls. at 236 m.p.h. at 20,000 ft. at 75% power; initial climb, 1,610 ft./min.; service ceil. 26,180 ft.

Weights: Empty, 3,719 lb.; max. take-off, 6,300 lb.

Accommodation: Flight crew of one or two with individual seats for eight passengers on each side of central aisle. Seats readily removable for freight operations.

Status: Model 402 announced on November 1, 1966, 133 having been delivered by beginning of 1969. Improved Model 402-A announced on February 19, 1969 with production deliveries shortly afterwards.

Notes: Model 402-A differs from initial model in having an extended nose providing a 600-lb. capacity baggage compartment and optional separate entry door for pilot. The Model 402-A differs from the Model 401-A in having the lengthened nose and convertible interior. The latter is a six–eight seat business executive transport with an essentially similar airframe.

60

CESSNA MODEL 402-A

Dimensions: Span, 39 ft. 10⅓ in.; length, 36 ft. 1 in.;
height, 11 ft. 8 in.; wing area, 195·7 sq. ft.

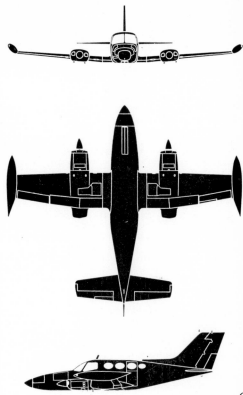

CESSNA MODEL 500 CITATION

Country of Origin: U.S.A.

Type: Light executive transport.

Power Plants: Two Pratt & Whitney JT15D-1 turbofans each rated at 2,200 lb.s.t.

Performance: (At 9,500 lb.) Max. speed, 406 m.p.h. at 26,400 ft.; max. cruise, 403 m.p.h. at 25,400 ft.; range (at 10,350 lb. with seven persons, normal allowances and 45 min. reserves) at max. cruise thrust, 1,052 mls. at 30,000 ft., 1,215 mls. at 35,000 ft., at 90% max. cruise thrust, 1,117 mls. at 30,000 ft., 1,280 mls. at 35,000 ft.; initial climb, 3,630 ft./min. at 9,500 lb., 3,260 ft./min. at 10,350 lb.

Weights: Empty, 5,408 lb.; max. take-off, 10,350 lb.

Accommodation: Normal flight crew of one or two and standard seating arrangement for four reclining seats plus corner bench seat behind co-pilot.

Status: Prototype flown September 15, 1969 with first production deliveries scheduled to commence August 1971, and eight per month planned for 1972.

Notes: Originally projected as the Fanjet 500 (see 1969 edition), the Citation is claimed to be capable of operating at light weight from fields as short as 2,500 ft. The second prototype was scheduled to fly in January 1970, and it is anticipated that some 20 demonstration aircraft will be produced in 1971, approximately 10 being delivered to customers in the same year. Two versions are to be offered, a basic version without avionics and a business version with factory-installed avionics.

CESSNA MODEL 500 CITATION

Dimensions: Span, 43 ft. 8⅔ in.; length, 44 ft. 5⅜ in.; height, 14 ft. 3¾ in.

CESSNA A-37B

Country of Origin: U.S.A.

Type: Two-seat light strike and counter-insurgency aircraft.

Power Plants: Two General Electric J85-GE-17A turbojets each rated at 2,850 lb.s.t.

Performance: Max. speed (without external stores), 478 m.p.h. at sea level, 507 m.p.h. at 16,000 ft., (with full external stores), 436 m.p.h. at sea level; initial climb (at 12,000 lb.), 6,990 ft./min., (at 8,000 lb.), 10,000 ft./min.; combat radius (pilot only, 12,000 lb. gross weight, cruise at 25,000 ft. with 10 min. single-engine loiter at 15,000 ft. and 5 min. combat at sea level), 85 mls. with 4,700 lb. ordnance, 250 mls. with 3,700 lb., and 550 mls. with 1,300 lb.; service ceil., 41,765 ft.; max. range, 1,012 mls.

Weights: Empty, 5,843 lb.; max. loaded, 14,000 lb.

Armament: One 7·62-mm. Minigun in fuselage nose and maximum of 5,680 lb. of ordnance (pilot only).

Status: In production. Thirty-nine A-37As delivered May–September 1967, followed by first A-37Bs from May 1968. Contracts for 327 A-37Bs for 1968–70 delivery placed by the beginning of 1970.

Notes: The A-37A is modified from airframe of T-37B trainer, has 2,400 lb.s.t. engines, and after evaluation in Vietnam by U.S.A.F. 604th Air Commando Squadron entered service in April 1969 with the V.N.A.F. 524th Fighter Squadron. The A-37B has uprated engines and provision for in-flight refuelling.

CESSNA A-37B

Dimensions: Span (over tip-tanks), 35 ft. 10½ in.; length, (over refuelling probe), 31 ft. 4 in.; height, 9 ft. 2 in.; wing area, 183·9 sq. ft.

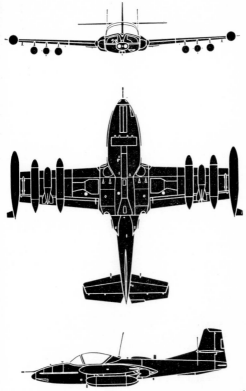

DASSAULT FALCON F (MYSTÈRE 20)

Country of Origin: France.
Type: Light business executive transport.
Power Plants: Two General Electric CF700-2D turbofans each rated at 4,250 lb.s.t.
Performance: Max. cruise, 535 m.p.h. at 25,000 ft.; econ. cruise, 466 m.p.h. at 40,000 ft.; range (normal allowances, a 1,600-lb. payload and 45 min. reserves), 1,870 mls. at 466 m.p.h. at 40,000 ft., 1,400 mls. at 520 m.p.h. at 25,000 ft.; max. range, 2,235 mls.
Weights: Empty equipped, 15,840 lb.; max. take-off, 28,660 lb.
Accommodation: Normal flight crew of two and standard arrangement for eight passengers in individual seats. Alternative arrangements available for 10–14 passengers.
Status: Current production Falcon F (Mystère 20 Modèle 70) of which prototype (172nd airframe) flown May 1969, customer deliveries being scheduled to commence early 1970. Total of 202 Falcons delivered against orders for 269 by beginning of October 1969.
Notes: The Falcon F (known in France as the Mystère 20 Modèle 70) differs from the preceding production version (Modèle 68) in having a full-span leading-edge high-lift system—Krüger-type slat inboard and slotted slat outboard—to reduce field length, and uprated turbofans. A proposed development for 1972 delivery (Modèle 72) will have Garrett AiResearch ATF-3 turbofans and transcontinental range.

DASSAULT FALCON F (MYSTÈRE 20)

Dimensions: Span, 53 ft. 6 in.; length, 56 ft. 3 in.;
height, 17 ft. 5 in.; wing area, 440 sq. ft.

DASSAULT MD 320 HIRONDELLE

Country of Origin: France.
Type: Light business executive and utility transport.
Power Plants: Two Turboméca Astazou XIV turbo-props each rated at 870 e.h.p.
Performance: (Estimated with Astazou XVI engines) at 12,236 lb.) Max. cruise, 280 m.p.h.; long-range cruise, 221 m.p.h.; range at max. cruise (normal allowances and 45 min. reserves), 1,925 mls.; time to 20,000 ft., 13 min.; service ceil., 30,850 ft.
Weights: Operational empty, 7,716 lb.; max. take-off 12,236 lb.
Accommodation: Normal flight crew of one or two, and alternative arrangements for six executive-type seats, eight, ten or twelve passengers in airliner-type seating or 14 passengers in high-density configuration.
Status: Prototype flown on September 11, 1968. No definitive production plans announced at time of closing for press.
Notes: The Hirondelle was designed primarily to meet an *Armée de l'Air* requirement for a turboprop-powered aircrew trainer and communications aircraft which was subsequently dropped in favour of a pure jet aircraft. In consequence, the Hirondelle is now being aimed primarily at the commercial market, the proposed production version having 1,088 e.h.p. Astazou XVIs.

DASSAULT MD 320 HIRONDELLE

Dimensions: Span, 47 ft. 8¾ in.; length, 40 ft. 2¼ in.; wing area, 290·62 sq. ft.

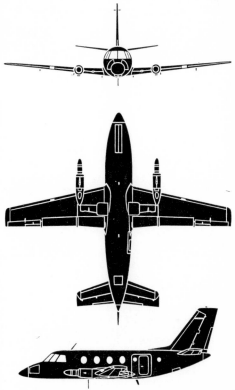

DASSAULT MERCURE

Country of Origin: France.

Type: Short-haul commercial transport.

Power Plants: Two Pratt & Whitney JT8D-11 turbofans each rated at 15,000 lb.s.t.

Performance: (Estimated at 109,130 lb.) Max. cruise, 576 m.p.h. at 22,000 ft.; range (24,000-lb. payload, max. fuel and normal reserves), 933 mls., (33,500-lb. payload), 400 mls.

Weights: Empty, 56,060 lb.; max. take-off, 109,000 lb.

Accommodation: Normal flight crew of two and high-density arrangement for 155 passengers in six-abreast seating with alternative arrangements for 134 economy-class or 16 first-class and 100 economy-class passengers.

Status: First prototype scheduled to fly late 1970 or early 1971 with first production aircraft being delivered late 1972 or early 1973. Two prototypes and two static test specimens under construction at beginning of 1970.

Notes: The Mercure is being developed under a multinational co-operative programme with Italy, Belgium, Spain and Switzerland participating. A French domestic carrier, Air Inter, took the first options on the Mercure in September 1969, covering the delivery of five aircraft in 1973 and five in 1974. Possessing a wider body than any current commercial transport of comparable size, the Mercure is claimed to offer exceptional short-field characteristics, and is optimised for use over very short ranges.

70

DASSAULT MERCURE

Dimensions: Span, 100 ft. 3 in.; length, 111 ft. 6 in.; height, 37 ft. 3 in.; wing area, 1,250 sq. ft.

DASSAULT FALCON 10 (MYSTÈRE 10)

Country of Origin: France.
Type: Light business executive transport.
Power Plants: Two SNECMA/Turboméca Larzac turbofans each rated at 2,304 lb.s.t., or two General Electric CJ610-9 turbofans of 3,100 lb.s.t., or two Garrett AiResearch TFE 731-2 turbofans each rated at 3,400 lb.s.t.
Performance: (Estimated with Larzac) Max. cruise (at 11,020 lb.), 513 m.p.h. at 36,000 ft.; econ. cruise, 460 m.p.h.; range (with normal allowances and reserves), 1,985 mls. at 460 m.p.h.
Weights: Empty equipped, 8,100 lb.; approx. max. take-off, 13,600 lb.
Accommodation: Normal flight crew of two plus up to seven passengers in individual seats. Alternative cabin arrangement for four passengers.
Status: First prototype scheduled to fly late summer of 1970 with initial production deliveries in 1972.
Notes: The Falcon 10 is to be offered on the commercial market with a choice of three power plants (listed above), and is competing with the SN 600 Corvette (see pages 220–221) for an *Armée de l'Air* for a crew trainer and light communications aircraft.

72

DASSAULT FALCON 10 (MYSTÈRE 10)

Dimensions: Span, 43 ft. 8½ in.; length, 44 ft. 5½ in.; height, 14 ft. 5¼ in.; wing area, 237 sq. ft.

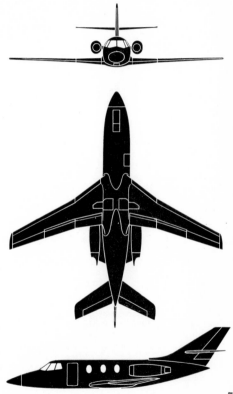

DASSAULT MIRAGE 5

Country of Origin: France.
Type: Single-seat tactical fighter-bomber.
Power Plant: One SNECMA Atar 9C turbojet rated at
9,436 lb.s.t. and 13,624 lb.s.t. with afterburning.
Performance: Max. speed, 875 m.p.h. at sea level
(Mach 1·15), 1,386 m.p.h. at 40,000 ft. (Mach 2·1);
range cruise, 594 m.p.h. at 36,000 ft. (Mach 0·9);
endurance (max. external fuel), 4 hr.
Weights: Empty equipped, 14,550 lb.; max. loaded,
29,760 lb.
Armament: Two 30-mm. DEFA 5-52 cannon plus
more than 8,800 lb. external ordnance. Typical load
for short-range interdiction mission comprises two
1,000-lb., ten 500-lb. and two 250-lb. bombs, plus two
110 Imp. gal. auxiliary fuel tanks.
Status: In production. Deliveries initiated (to Peru)
mid-1968.
Notes: The Mirage M5 is an export version of the
Mirage IIIE (see 1967 edition) optimised for the
ground attack role and featuring simplified avionics.
Fifty ordered by Israel (Mirage 5-J) and completed
mid-1969, but embargo placed by French government
on delivery. Twelve (Mirage 5-P) delivered to Peru
and 106 ordered by Belgium of which 59 (Mirage 5-BA)
for ground attack, 31 (Mirage 5-BR) for tactical
reconnaissance, and 16 as two-seaters (Mirage 5-BD)
for training. The Mirage M5 differs from the IIIE
basically in having the fire control radar, Doppler and
TACAN deleted.

DASSAULT MIRAGE 5

Dimensions: Span, 26 ft. 11½ in.; length, 52 ft. 0¼ in.; height, 13 ft. 11½ in.; wing area, 375·12 sq. ft.

DASSAULT MIRAGE F1

Country of Origin: France.

Type: Single-seat interceptor and strike fighter.

Power Plant: One SNECMA Atar 9K-50 turbojet rated at 11,067 lb.s.t. and 15,785 lb.s.t. with afterburning.

Performance: Max. speed, 1,450 m.p.h. at 40,000 ft. (Mach 2·2), 915 m.p.h. at sea level (Mach 1·2); long-range cruise, 550 m.p.h. at 30,000 ft.; max. range (with max. external fuel), 2,050 mls.; service ceil. 65,700 ft.

Weights: Empty, 16,425 lb.; empty equipped (including pilot), 24,030 lb.; loaded (without external stores), 25,350 lb.; max., 32,630 lb.

Armament: Two 30-mm. DEFA cannon and (intercept) two Matra R.530 and two AIM-9 Sidewinder AAMs, or (attack) max. of 14 250-lb. bombs, or mix of conventional ordnance, including Martel or AS.30 ASMs.

Status: First prototype flown December 23, 1966, and second and third on March 29 and September 18, 1969 respectively. Contract for initial quantity of 35 placed May 1969 with first deliveries scheduled for early 1971.

Notes: Intended as a successor to the Mirage III in *Armée de l'Air* service, the Mirage F1 is primarily an all-weather all-altitude interceptor but is also suitable for the attack role. Unlike previous aircraft in the Mirage series which have featured tailless delta configuration, the F1 has a swept wing and conventional tail, and variants proposed include a less sophisticated export model (F1A) and the two-seat F1B.

76

DASSAULT MIRAGE F1

Dimensions: Span, 27 ft. 6¾ in.; length, 49 ft. 2½ in.; height, 14 ft. 9 in.; wing area, 269 sq. ft.

DASSAULT MIRAGE G

Country of Origin: France.

Type: Two-seat strike and reconnaissance fighter.

Power Plant: One SNECMA TF-306E turbofan rated at 11,684 lb.s.t. and 20,503 lb.s.t. with afterburning.

Performance: (Estimated) Max. speed, 840 m.p.h. at sea level (Mach 1·1), 1,650 m.p.h. at 40,000 ft. (Mach 2·5); initial climb rate, 35,000 ft./min.; endurance (max. external fuel at econ. cruise), 8 hr.; service ceil., 65,000 ft.; ferry range, 4,000 mls.

Weights: Empty, 22,500 lb.; loaded, 33,500 lb.

Armament: (Mirage G4) Conventional or nuclear stores on six external stations, and two 30-mm. cannon internally.

Status: Experimental. First prototype flown October 18, 1967. Two prototypes of twin-engined derivative (Mirage G4) ordered September 1968, with first scheduled to fly December 1970.

Notes: Essentially a variable-geometry equivalent of the Mirage F2 (see 1967 edition), the Mirage G is currently under development to provide a strike and reconnaissance fighter for *Armée de l'Air* use from 1975. The Mirage G's wing is swept 20° when fully extended and 70° in the full aft position, and translates from full forward to full aft in approximately 20 seconds. Mirage G4 derivative will be powered by two Atar 9K-50 turbojets, will be larger than the current prototype, and will have clean and max. loaded weights of the order of 44,090 lb. and 55,120 lb.

78

DASSAULT MIRAGE G

Dimensions: Span (maximum sweep), 22 ft. $11\frac{1}{2}$ in.;
(minimum sweep), 49 ft. $2\frac{1}{2}$ in.; length, 55 ft. $1\frac{1}{2}$ in.;
height, 17 ft. $6\frac{1}{2}$ in.

DE HAVILLAND CANADA DHC-5 BUFFALO

Country of Origin: Canada.

Type; Military tactical and utility transport.

Power Plants: Two General Electric T64-GE-14 turboprops each rated at 3,060 e.s.h.p.

Performance: Max. speed, 282 m.p.h. at 10,000 ft.; cruise, at 80% power, 253 m.p.h., at 52% power, 208 m.p.h.; initial climb, 2,080 ft./min.; service ceil., 31,500 ft.; range (with 12,780 lb.), 553 mls., (with 8,000 lb.), 1,300 mls., (with 4,000 lb.), 1,958 mls., (max. fuel, no payload), 2,142 mls.

Weights: Operational empty, 24,220 lb.; max. take-off, 41,000 lb.

Accommodation: Crew of three plus 41 troops, 35 paratroops, or 24 casualty stretchers.

Status: In production. First of four evaluation aircraft (CV-7) flown April 9, 1964. Deliveries against initial order for 15 (CC-115) for Canadian Armed Forces' Mobile Command commenced 1967. Twelve for Brazilian Air Force delivered 1968, and second batch of 12 delivered 1969.

Notes: Originally designed primarily to meet a U.S. Army requirement. Four delivered to this service of which three survivors transferred in 1967 to NASA when U.S.A.F. assumed responsibility for fixed-wing intra-theatre airlift.

80

DE HAVILLAND CANADA DHC-5 BUFFALO

Dimensions: Span, 96 ft. 0 in.; length, 79 ft. 0 in.; height, 28 ft. 8 in.; wing area, 945 sq. ft.

DE HAVILLAND CANADA DHC-6
TWIN OTTER SERIES 300

Country of Origin: Canada.

Type: STOL utility transport and feederliner.

Power Plants: Two Pratt & Whitney PT6A-27 turbo-props each rated at 652 e.s.h.p.

Performance: (At 12,500 lb.) Max. cruise, 202 m.p.h. at 10,000 ft.; range at max. cruise (with 3,250-lb. payload), 710 mls., (with 13 passengers and 45 min. reserves), 806 mls., (with 20 passengers, fuel reserve for 115-mile diversion and 45 min. hold), 680 mls.; initial climb, 1,440 ft./min.; service ceil., 25,000 ft.

Weights: Empty equipped (13 passengers), 6,610 lb., (20 passengers), 7,250 lb.; max. take-off, 12,500 lb.

Accommodation: Normal flight crew of one or two, and seats for up to 20 passengers in main cabin. Freighter, executive, survey or ambulance interiors available.

Status: First of five pre-production (Srs. 100) aircraft flown May 20, 1965. The 231st aircraft off the assembly line was first Srs. 300 of which deliveries commenced spring 1969.

Notes: The Srs. 300 Twin Otter is externally similar to the Srs. 200 (extended aft baggage compartment and lengthened nose) introduced April 1968 apart from the power plants, all earlier models having 579 e.s.h.p. PT6A-20A turboprops. The Twin Otter is also available as a twin-float seaplane.

82

DE HAVILLAND CANADA DHC-6
TWIN OTTER SERIES 300

Dimensions: Span, 65 ft. 0 in.; length, 51 ft. 9 in.; height, 18 ft. 7 in.; wing area, 420 sq. ft.

DORNIER D-2 SKYSERVANT

Country of Origin: Federal Germany.
Type: Light STOL freighter and feederliner.
Power Plants: Two Lycoming IGSO-540-A1E six-cylinder horizontally-opposed engines each rated at 380 h.p.
Performance: (At 8,050 lb.) Max. speed, 199 m.p.h. at 10,500 ft.; cruise (75% power), 161 m.p.h. at sea level, 169 m.p.h. at 5,000 ft., 177 m.p.h. at 10,000 ft., (65% power), 152 m.p.h. at sea level, 161 m.p.h. at 5,000 ft., 167 m.p.h. at 10,000 ft.; max. range, 1,143 mls. at 143 m.p.h. at 10,000 ft.; initial climb, 1,180 ft./min.; service ceil., 24,300 ft.
Weights: Empty, 4,620 lb.; max. take-off, 8,050 lb.
Accommodation: Pilot and 8–14 passengers.
Status: In production. First of three prototypes flown February 23, 1966, an output of four per month being attained by mid-1968. Production rate raised to 6–8 per month 1969.
Notes: Capable of operation from skis and floats, the Skyservant places accent on ease of maintenance and 125 are to be delivered to the *Luftwaffe* and *Marineflieger*. Four of the aircraft to be delivered to the *Luftwaffe* will be employed for governmental transportation purposes, and the remaining 101 for photo survey, ambulance and utility roles. The 20 *Marineflieger* aircraft will be used for search and rescue.

DORNIER D-2 SKYSERVANT

Dimensions: Span, 50 ft. 10¾ in.; length, 37 ft. 4¾ in.; height, 12 ft. 9½ in.; wing area, 308 sq. ft.

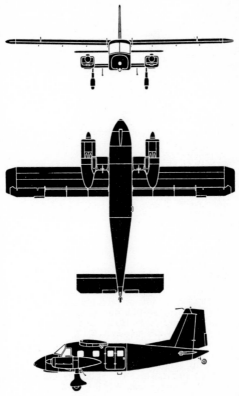

EMBRAER C-95 BANDEIRANTE

Country of Origin: Brazil.

Type: Light military utility transport.

Power Plants: Two Pratt & Whitney PT6A-20 turbo-props each rated at 579 e.s.h.p., or (production) PT6A-27 turboprops each rated at 652 e.s.h.p.

Performance: (PT6A-20 engines) Max. speed, 283 m.p.h. at 9,840 ft.; max. cruise, 263 m.p.h. at 9,840 ft.; range (with normal allowances and 30 min. reserves), 900 mls. at 9,840 ft., 1,137 mls. at 16,400 ft.; initial climb, 1,890 ft./min.; service ceil., 29,530 ft.

Weights: (PT6A-20) Empty equipped, 5,620 lb.; max. take-off, 9,920 lb.

Accommodation: Flight crew of two and nine passengers in individual seats. Production model will accommodate 12 passengers.

Status: First of four prototypes flown on October 22, 1968 and second in September 1969. Third prototype is scheduled to join test programme in June 1970, and the fourth, the production prototype, in October 1970. Production deliveries to commence in 1971.

Notes: Developed as the IPD-6504 by a division of the Centro Técnico de Aeronáutica, the Bandeirante is being manufactured by EMBRAER (Empresa Brasileira de Aeronáutica S.A.) for the Brazilian Air Force. The fourth prototype will be representative of the production model, with a 2 ft. 7½ in. increase in fuselage length, and deeper engine nacelles.

EMBRAER C-95 BANDEIRANTE

Dimensions: Span, 50 ft. 7 in.; length, 41 ft. 9½ in.;
height, 16 ft. 11½ in.; wing area, 374 sq. ft.

FIAT G.91Y

Country of Origin: Italy.

Type: Single-seat light strike and reconnaissance fighter.

Power Plants: Two General Electric J85-GE-13A turbojets each rated at 2,725 lb.s.t. and 4,080 lb.s.t. with afterburning.

Performance: Max. speed, 714 m.p.h. at sea level (Mach 0·94), 690 m.p.h. at 32,800 ft. (Mach. 0·975); range cruise at 500 ft., 380–405 m.p.h.; tactical radius (lo-lo-lo attack mission on internal fuel with 2,910-lb. military payload), 240 mls., (intercept mission with 2,635-lb. military payload), 265 mls.; ferry range with 10% reserves (two 57 Imp. gal. aux. tanks), 1,620 mls., (two 114 Imp. gal. tanks), 1,930 mls., (two 176 Imp. gal. tanks), 2,110 mls.; initial climb (at 15,000 lb.), 15,700 ft./min., max. climb (at 11,500 ft.), 16,700 ft./min.; service ceil., 41,200 ft.

Weights: Empty, 8,598 lb.; normal max., 17,196 lb.; max. overload, 19,180 lb.

Armament: Two 30-mm. DEFA 552 cannon and max. of 4,000 lb. of ordnance on four wing pylons.

Status: First prototype flown December 27, 1966, production prototype following September 1967. First of 20 pre-production aircraft flown summer 1969, followed by deliveries of 55 production examples from early 1970 at rate of three per month.

Notes: The G.91Y is to equip four *Aeronautica Militare* fighter-bomber squadrons.

FIAT G.91Y

Dimensions: Span, 29 ft. 6½ in.; length, 38 ft. 3½ in.; height, 14 ft. 6⅓ in.; wing area, 195·149 sq. ft.

FMA IA 58 DELFIN

Country of Origin: Argentina.

Type: Tandem two-seat light counter-insurgency aircraft.

Power Plants: Two Garrett AiResearch TPE 331-3U-303 turboprops each rated at 840 s.h.p.

Performance: (Estimated at 13,668 lb.) Max. speed, 308 m.p.h. at 9,840 ft.; max. cruise, 295 m.p.h. at 9,840 ft.; max. range, 2,235 mls.; service ceil. (at 11,464 lb.), 29,200 ft.

Weights: Empty, 7,826 lb.; max. loaded, 13,668 lb.

Armament: Various combinations of gun pods, bombs and rocket missiles on four underwing pylons, plus two 20-mm. cannon and four 7·62-mm. machine guns in fuselage.

Status: First prototype flown August 20, 1969 in powered form, flight trials having been initiated on December 26, 1967 in unpowered form with dummy engine nacelles. Planned production order for 80 aircraft for Argentine Air Force with deliveries commencing 1971–72.

Notes: The IA 58 counter-insurgency aircraft project was initiated in August 1966 by the Fábrica Militar de Aviones at Córdoba, which will also be responsible for the series production of the aircraft. Design of the IA 58 emphasises ease of maintenance and suitability for operation from short, unimproved strips. Pratt & Whitney PT6A turboprops are offered as alternative power plants.

FMA IA 58 DELFIN

Dimensions: Span, 47 ft. 3 in.; length, 43 ft. 11½ in.; height, 15 ft. 6 in.; wing area, 326·15 sq. ft.

FOKKER F.27 FRIENDSHIP SRS. 500

Country of Origin: Netherlands.
Type: Short- to medium-range commercial transport.
Power Plants: Two Rolls-Royce Dart 532-7 turbo-props each rated at 2,250 e.s.h.p.
Performance: Max. cruise, 322 m.p.h. at 20,000 ft.; long-range cruise, 291 m.p.h. at 20,000 ft.; range (max. fuel, 8,914-lb. payload and reserves), 1,135 mls.; range (with 10,950-lb. payload), 430 mls.; initial climb (at 40,000 lb.), 1,450 ft./min.
Weights: Empty, 24,650 lb.; operational empty, 25,380 lb.; max. take-off, 43,500 lb.
Accommodation: Basic flight crew of two or three, and alternative arrangements for 52 or 56 passengers.
Status: In production. First Friendship 500 flown November 15, 1967. Approximately 320 Friendships of all versions delivered by parent company by beginning of 1970.
Notes: By comparison with the Series 200 (see 1968 edition), the Series 500 has a 4 ft. 11 in. increase in fuselage length resulting from additional sections being inserted fore and aft of the wing. The large cargo door originally featured by the Series 400 "Combiplane" convertible cargo or combined cargo-and-freighter versions of the Series 200 is also used by the Series 500. This cargo door is also featured by the Series 600 which is otherwise similar to the Series 200, lacking the reinforced floor of the "Combiplane". A basically similar stretched version of the Friendship is manufactured under licence in the U.S.A. by Fairchild Hiller as the FH-227B (see 1968 edition).

FOKKER F.27 FRIENDSHIP SRS. 500

Dimensions: Span, 95 ft. 1¾ in.; length, 82 ft. 2½ in.; height, 28 ft. 7¼ in.; wing area, 754 sq. ft.

FOKKER F.28 FELLOWSHIP

Country of Origin: Netherlands.

Type: Short-haul commercial transport.

Power Plants: Two Rolls-Royce RB.183-2 Mk. 555-15 Spey Junior turbofans each rated at 9,850 lb.s.t.

Performance: Max. cruise, 527 m.p.h. at 21,000 ft.; econ. cruise 519 m.p.h. at 25,000 ft.; long-range cruise, 426 m.p.h.; range (with 60 passengers and 10% reserves), 1,160 mls. at 30,000 ft.

Weights: Operational empty, 33,800 lb.; max. take-off, 62,000 lb.

Accommodation: Alternative arrangements for 40 passengers in first-class seating four abreast, or 55, 60 or 65 passengers in five-abreast all-tourist seating.

Status: In production. First of three prototypes flown May 9, 1967, and first production aircraft flown on May 21, 1968. First production delivery (to Braathens S.A.F.E.) on March 3, 1969, and 29 ordered by December 1969.

Notes: The F.28 Fellowship is a European co-operative effort in which the nose section is of Fokker design and production; fuselage section 1 is of Fokker design and VFW construction; fuselage sections 2 and 3 are of Fokker design and production; wing centre section is of Fokker design and production; outer wing is of Short Brothers design and production; fuselage section 4 and engine nacelles are of HFB design and construction, and the tail assembly is of VFW design and construction. The F.28 is being distributed in the U.S.A. by Fairchild Hiller, the fulfilment of an initial order for 10 having commenced in 1969.

FOKKER F.28 FELLOWSHIP

Dimensions: Span, 77 ft. 4¼ in.; length, 89 ft. 10¾ in.; height, 27 ft. 9½ in.; wing area, 822 sq. ft.

FUJI FA-200 AERO SUBARU

Country of Origin: Japan.

Type: Light cabin monoplane.

Power Plant: One Lycoming (FA-200-160) O-320-D2A or (FA-200-180) IO-360-B1B four-cylinder horizontally-opposed engine rated at 160 and 180 h.p. respectively.

Performance: (Specification applies to FA-200-160 with figures in parentheses relating to the FA-200-180) Max. speed, 139 (145) m.p.h. at sea level; max. cruise at 75% power at 5,000 ft., 122 (127) m.p.h.; econ. cruise at 55% power at 5,000 ft., 100 (108) m.p.h.; max. range, 740 (700) mls.; initial climb, 680 (760) ft./min.; service ceil., 11,400 (13,700) ft.

Weights: Empty, 1,247 (1,367) lb.; max. take-off, 2,337 (2,535) lb.

Accommodation: Four seats in side-by-side pairs.

Status: First prototype flown August 12, 1965, and followed by 10 pre-production aircraft. First production aircraft completed December 4, 1968. Initial batch of 46 followed by further 70 for completion by April 1970, a production rate of seven per month being attained by end of 1969.

Notes: The first Japanese four-seat light cabin monoplane to be manufactured in substantial numbers, the Aero Subaru is available in fully-aerobatic two-seat form with both 160 and 180 h.p. engines, and an experimental STOL version, the FA-203S with leading-edge slats and full-span trailing-edge "flaperons" and other high-lift devices is used by the Japanese National Aerospace Laboratory.

96

FUJI FA-200 AERO SUBARU

Dimensions: Span, 30 ft. 11 in.; length, 26 ft. 1 in.; height, 8 ft. 7½ in.; wing area, 150·7 sq. ft.

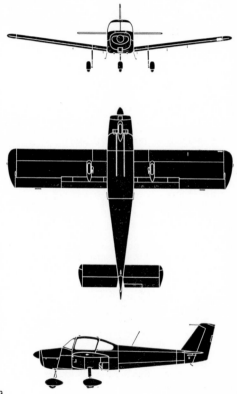

GENERAL DYNAMICS F-111E

Country of Origin: U.S.A.

Type: Two-seat tactical strike fighter.

Power Plants: Two Pratt & Whitney TF30-P-3 turbo-fans each rated at (approx.) 12,000 lb.s.t. and 20,000 lb.s.t. with full afterburning.

Performance: Max. speed, 1,650 m.p.h. at 40,000 ft. (Mach 2·5), 865 m.p.h. at sea level (Mach 1·2); range (max. internal fuel), 3,800–4,000 mls.; tactical radius (hi-lo-hi mission profile with 16,000-lb. combat load), 1,500–1,700 mls.; max. climb (approx. at 74,000 lb.), 40,000 ft./min.

Weights: Empty operational, 47,500 lb.; normal loaded, 74,000 lb.; max. overload, 91,500 lb.

Armament: One 20-mm. M-61A1 rotary cannon with 2,000 rounds or two 750-lb. M117 bombs in weapons bay and various ordnance loads up to some 30,000 lb. on four swivelling 4,000-lb. capacity wing stations and (subsonic missions) four fixed wing stations of similar capacity.

Status: First F-111 flown December 21, 1964. One hundred and forty-one F-111As being followed by 94 F-111Es from late 1969. These to be followed by 96 F-111Ds, prototype of which flown September 1969, and subsequent aircraft (from 332nd) will be F-111Fs.

Notes: F-111E differs from F-111A in having revised engine intake geometry, and F-111D will be similar but will carry more advanced (Mk. 2) avionics. F-111F will have 25,000 lb.s.t. TF-30-P-100 engines and simpler avionics.

GENERAL DYNAMICS F-111E

Dimensions: Span (minimum sweep), 63 ft. 0 in., (maximum sweep), 31 ft. 11⅓ in.; length, 73 ft. 6 in.; height, 17 ft. 1⅓ in.

GENERAL DYNAMICS FB-111A

Country of Origin: U.S.A.
Type: Two-seat strategic bomber.
Power Plants: Two Pratt & Whitney TF30-P-7 turbo-fans each rated at (approx.) 12,500 lb.s.t. and 21,000 lb.s.t. with full afterburning.
Performance: Max. speed (clean configuration), 1,450 m.p.h. at 40,000 ft. (Mach 2·2), 838 m.p.h. at sea level (Mach 1·1); range (subsonic cruise to target, supersonic final approach and escape, and return at subsonic speed on internal fuel, carrying four SRAM to target area), 2,500 mls.; max. range (with four 500-Imp. gal. auxiliary tanks on underwing pylons), 4,100 mls.; service ceil., 65,000 ft.
Weights: Approx. max. loaded, 100,000 lb.
Armament: Up to six 2,200-lb. Boeing AGM-69A short-range attack missiles (SRAM) on external pylons, or conventional ordnance loads up to 37,500 lb. (e.g., 50 750-lb. bombs on multiple ejection racks).
Status: First FB-111A flown July 13, 1968, and first delivered to U.S.A.F. Strategic Air Command on October 8, 1969. Total of 76 to be manufactured.
Notes: The FB-111A is a hybrid aircraft in having an essentially similar airframe to the F-111E (see pages 98–99) with its so-called "Triple Plow 2" engine air intake arrangement, the long-span wing of the now-defunct shipboard F-111B, and a Mk. 2B avionics system basically similar to that of the F-111D. To these features are added a strengthened undercarriage to cater for increased overload weights, and higher-thrust engines.

GENERAL DYNAMICS FB-111A

Dimensions: Span, (minimum sweep), 70 ft. 0 in., (maximum sweep), 33 ft. 11 in.; length, 73 ft. 6 in.; height, 17 ft. 0 in.

GRUMMAN A-6A INTRUDER

Country of Origin: U.S.A.

Type: Two-seat shipboard low-level strike aircraft.

Power Plants: Two Pratt & Whitney J52-P-8A turbojets each rated at 9,300 lb.s.t.

Performance: Max. speed (at 36,655 lb.), 685 m.p.h. at sea level (Mach 0·9), 625 m.p.h. at 36,000 ft., (at 60,280 lb. for close support mission with 30 500-lb. Mk. 82 bombs), 568 m.p.h. at sea level; range (max. internal fuel and four Bullpup ASMs), 1,920 mls. at average cruise of 477 m.p.h. at 36,600–43,000 ft., (with single store and four 250 Imp. gal. external tanks), 3,040 mls. at average cruise of 481 m.p.h. at 32,750–43,800 ft.

Weights: Empty, 25,684 lb.; loaded (clean), 37,116 lb.; max. overload, 60,280 lb.

Armament: Maximum external ordnance load of 15,000 lb. on five 3,600-lb. capacity stores stations.

Status: First of eight test and evaluation aircraft flown April 19, 1960 followed by first delivery to U.S. Navy on February 7, 1963. Approx. 450 delivered by beginning of 1970.

Notes: A-6B is modification of A-6A as a special-purpose missile carrier, conversions being undertaken at Pomono Modification Center. A-6B carries such missiles as AGM-78A Standard ARM. A-6C is version of A-6A with special electro-optical sensors, KA-6D is shipboard tanker version, 20 of which are being produced for 1970 delivery, and A-6E is updated version of A-6A with new radar and computer for 1971 delivery.

GRUMMAN A-6A INTRUDER

Dimensions: Span, 53 ft. 0 in.; length, 54 ft. 7 in.; height, 15 ft. 7 in.; wing area, 529 sq. ft.

GRUMMAN F-14A

Country of Origin: U.S.A.

Type: Two-seat shipboard multi-purpose fighter.

Power Plants: Two Pratt & Whitney TF30-P-401 turbofans each rated at (approx.) 23,000 lb.s.t. with full afterburning.

Performance: Max. speed (intercept mission with four AIM-7 Sparrow AAMs at approx. 50,000 lb.), 1,650 m.p.h. at 60,000 ft. (Mach 2·5), 865 m.p.h. at sea level (Mach 1·2).

Weights: Approx. operational empty, 35,000 lb.; approx. normal loaded, 50,000 lb.

Armament: One 20-mm. M-61A1 rotary cannon and maximum missile loads of six AIM-7 Sparrow or six AIM-54A Phoenix AAMs plus four AIM-9 Sidewinder AAMs, four of the Sparrows or Phoenixes being carried semi-submerged in base of fuselage and two being carried beneath the engine nacelles on ejector racks, the four Sidewinders being carried on pylons outboard of the nacelles. For the attack role 250-lb., 500-lb., or 1,000-lb. bombs may be carried.

Status: First of six development and test F-14s scheduled to be rolled out December 1970 and flown January 1971. U.S. Navy has an option for procurement of 463 F-14A and F-14B aircraft, the former being scheduled to attain operational status 1973.

Notes: Variable geometry wing with 20 deg. sweep in full forward position and 68 deg. in full aft position. F-14B is follow-on version with more powerful engines.

GRUMMAN F-14A

Dimensions: No details available at time of closing for press.

HAL HJT-16 KIRAN

Country of Origin: India.
Type: Two-seat basic trainer.
Power Plant: One Rolls-Royce Bristol Viper 11 turbo-jet rated at 2,500 lb.s.t.
Performance: Max. speed (at 7,712 lb.), 446 m.p.h. at sea level, 441 m.p.h. at 30,000 ft.; range cruise, 230 m.p.h. at 20,000 ft.; range (internal fuel), 480 mls., (with two 50 Imp. gal. auxiliary tanks), 660 mls.
Weights: Empty, 5,362 lb.; normal loaded, 7,712 lb.; max. loaded, 8,660 lb.
Status: First prototype flown September 4, 1964, and second in August 1965. Delivery of 24 pre-production examples initiated March 1968, and the first production examples were expected to be completed late 1969.
Notes: Development of the Kiran was initiated in 1958 under the leadership of Dr. V. M. Ghatage, and design proposals were approved in December 1959, the aircraft being intended as an indigenous successor to the Vampire T. Mk. 55. Initial contracts call for 24 Viper-powered pre-production aircraft and 36 production aircraft powered by the indigenous HJE-2500 turbojet which, rated at 2,500 lb.s.t., first ran in December 1966, series production being initiated in 1969. The HJE-2500-powered Kiran is expected to have an essentially similar performance to that of the Viper-engined model, and orders currently planned are expected to raise the total number of Kirans built to some 170.

HAL HJT-16 KIRAN

Dimensions: Span, 35 ft. 1¼ in.; length, 34 ft. 9 in.; height, 11 ft. 11 in.; wing area, 204·5 sq. ft.

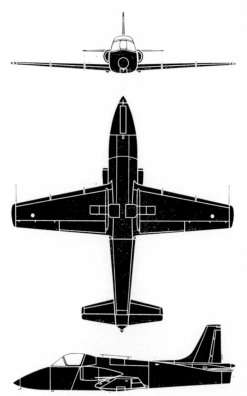

HANDLEY PAGE JETSTREAM 3M

Country of Origin: United Kingdom.
Type: Light business executive and utility transport.
Power Plants: Two Garrett AiResearch TPE 331-3W-301A turboprops each rated at 840 s.h.p.
Performance: Max. cruise (at 14,000 lb.), 288 m.p.h. at 15,000 ft.; range (max. fuel with 5% reserves plus allowances for 45 min. hold), 2,487 mls., (with 12 passengers and similar reserves), 950 mls.; initial climb, 420 ft./min.; service ceil. (at 13,500 lb.), 27,000 ft.
Weights: Max. take-off, 14,500 lb.
Accommodation: Normal flight crew of two and various alternative interior arrangements for eight to 12 passengers.
Status: First prototype Jetstream flown August 18, 1967, and first prototype Jetstream 3M on November 21, 1968. First production example (Jetstream 1) flown December 6, 1968. Production switched to Jetstream 2 late 1969 after completion of 30th Jetstream 1.
Notes: The Jetstream suffered weight and drag problems during early development, resulting in delivery delays while modifications were introduced and substantial increases in price. One result of these difficulties has been the production phase-out of the Jetstream 1 (see 1969 edition) with 850 e.s.h.p. Turboméca Astazou XIVCs in favour of the Jetstream 2 with 1,073 e.s.h.p. Astazou XVIs, another being the cancellation by the U.S.A.F. of a batch of 11 Jetstream 3Ms. Production is now standardising on the Astazou-powered Jetstream 2, but the TPE 331-powered Jetstream 3 is likely to be offered on the U.S. market.

HANDLEY PAGE JETSTREAM 3M

Dimensions: Span, 52 ft. 0 in.; length, 47 ft. 1½ in.; height, 17 ft. 5½ in.; wing area, 270 sq. ft.

HANDLEY PAGE VICTOR B.(S.R.) MK. 2

Country of Origin: United Kingdom.

Type: Long-range strategic reconnaissance and surveillance aircraft.

Power Plants: Four Rolls-Royce Conway R.Co.17 Mk. 201 turbofans each rated at 19,750 lb.s.t.

Performance: (Estimated) Max. speed, 630 m.p.h. at 36,000–50,000 ft. (Mach 0·95); max. cruise, 610 m.p.h. at 55,000 ft.; long-range cruise, 560 m.p.h. at 40,000 ft. (Mach 0·85); radius of action (high-altitude mission), 2,300–2,500 mls.; max. range (with underwing and weapons bay tanks), 5,500–6,000 mls.

Weight: Max. loaded, 200,000 lb.

Accommodation: Crew of five in pressurised nose compartment. Camera equipment housed in packs mounted in the weapons bay, these packs accommodating a wide variety of camera combinations for day and night reconnaissance and aerial survey. In addition to a camera pack, the weapons bay can house three canisters containing a total of 108 photoflashes, or two photoflash canisters and an auxiliary fuel tank.

Status: Production completed by conversion of B. Mk. 2s to B.(S.R.) Mk. 2s was continuing in 1970.

Notes: The B.(S.R.) Mk. 2 is essentially similar to the B. Mk. 2 (see 1966 edition) phased out in 1968 and can be reconverted for the bombing role. The B.(S.R.) Mk. 2 is employed principally for high-altitude maritime patrol, and an in-flight processing unit produces continuous film map strips of the radar displays.

110

HANDLEY PAGE VICTOR B.(S.R.) MK. 2

Dimensions: Span, 120 ft. 0 in.; length 114 ft. 11 in.;
height, 30 ft. $1\frac{1}{2}$ in.; wing area, 2,597 sq. ft.

HAWKER SIDDELEY 125 SERIES 400

Country of Origin: United Kingdom.

Type: Light business executive transport.

Power Plants: Two Rolls-Royce Bristol Viper 522 turbojets each rated at 3,360 lb.s.t.

Performance: Max. cruise, 510 m.p.h. at 31,000 ft.; econ. cruise, 450 m.p.h. above 37,000 ft.; range (max. fuel and 1,940-lb. payload, no reserves), 1,940 mls., (1,000-lb. payload and reserves for 45 min. hold), 1,762 mls.; initial climb, 3,700 ft./min.; service ceil., 41,000 ft.

Weights: Empty equipped, 11,275 lb.; max. take-off, 23,300 lb.

Accommodation: Normal flight crew of two and standard cabin interior for seven passengers with alternative interior layouts for from six to 12 passengers.

Status: First HS 125 flown August 13, 1962, and first HS 125 Series 400 (actually the 173rd HS 125 built) on August 23, 1968. Deliveries of the Series 400 commenced early 1969, and 200 HS 125s had been completed by October of that year.

Notes: The HS 125 Series 400 represents a refinement of the Series 3AR (see 1968 edition), incorporating an outward-opening integral airstair door which increases baggage space, an aerodynamically-improved ventral fuselage fairing forward of the wing, and structural changes permitting a 500-lb. increase in maximum take-off weight. The Series 400A and 400B differ primarily in equipment standards. The navigational training version of the HS 125 for the R.A.F. is known as the Dominic T. Mk. 1.

HAWKER SIDDELEY 125 SERIES 400

Dimensions: Span, 47 ft. 0 in.; length, 47 ft. 5 in.; height, 16 ft. 6 in.; wing area, 353 sq. ft.

H

HAWKER SIDDELEY 748 SERIES 2A

Country of Origin: United Kingdom.
Type: Short- and medium-range commercial transport.
Power Plants: Two Rolls-Royce Dart R.Da.7 Mk. 532-2L turboprops each rated at 2,290 e.s.h.p.
Performance: Max. speed, 312 m.p.h. at 16,000 ft.; max. cruise, 277 m.p.h. at 15,000 ft.; econ. cruise, 267 m.p.h. at 20,000 ft.; range cruise, 259 m.p.h. at 25,000 ft.; initial climb, 1,150 ft./min.; range (with max. fuel and 6,985-lb. payload), 1,957 mls. at 273 m.p.h. at 20,000 ft., (with max. payload of 11,512 lb. and no reserves), 1,134 mls. at 267 m.p.h. at 20,000 ft.
Weights: Empty, 24,572 lb.; basic operational, 25,988 lb.; max. take-off, 44,495 lb.
Accommodation: Crew of two plus cabin attendants, and standard cabin arrangements for 40 passengers. High-density arrangements for 52 or 58 passengers.
Status: In production. First prototype flown June 24, 1960. First production aircraft (Srs. 1) flown August 30, 1961. Eighteen Srs. 1 aircraft delivered, plus four assembled in India by HAL for Indian Air Force. HAL is also producing 55 Srs. 2 aircraft. Approximately 180 delivered by end of 1969 when production rate was three aircraft per month.
Notes: Series 2A introduced in 1968 with uprated engines and various interior refinements.

114

HAWKER SIDDELEY 748 SERIES 2A

Dimensions: Span, 98 ft. 6 in.; length, 67 ft. 0 in.;
height, 24 ft. 10 in.; wing area, 810·75 sq. ft.

HAWKER SIDDELEY BUCCANEER S. MK.

Country of Origin: United Kingdom.

Type: Two-seat low-level strike aircraft.

Power Plants: Two Rolls-Royce RB.168-1A Spey R.Sp.2 Mk. 101 turbofans each rated at 11,000 lb.s.t.

Performance: (Estimated) Max. speed, 700 m.p.h. at sea level (Mach 0·92); max. low-level cruise, 665 m.p.h. at 5,000 ft. (Mach 0·9); long-range cruise, 575 m.p.h. at 33,000 ft. (Mach 0·83); tactical radius (without external fuel), 500–600 mls for hi-lo-lo-hi mission; ferry range (with two 250 Imp gal. underwing tanks and 750 Imp. gal. weapons-bay tank), 1,800–2000 mls.

Weights: Loaded (clean and without weapons), 42,000 lb.; max. 56,000 lb.

Armament: Four 1,000-lb. bombs or large single store in weapons bay, and additional offensive stores on four 1,000-lb. capacity underwing pylons. These pylons may each carry a Martel ASM, a 1,000-lb or 500-lb. bomb, 2-in. or 3-in. Glow worm rocket pack, 36-cell MATRA rocket dispenser, or AGM-12B ASM.

Status: In production. First of two Spey-powered pre-production aircraft flown May 17, 1963. First production S. Mk. 2 flown June 5, 1964. Delivery of 84 to R.N. completed December 1968, and production of 26 for R.A.F. scheduled to continue until 1971, with first delivery April 1970.

Notes: With the run-down of its carrier force, the Royal Navy is transferring some 70 Buccaneer S. Mk. 2s to the R.A.F. These are being modified to carry Martel missiles as S. Mk. 2Bs, and together with those now being built specifically for the R.A.F., will equip four Strike Command squadrons.

116

HAWKER SIDDELEY BUCCANEER S. MK. 2B

Dimensions: Span, 44 ft. 0 in.; length, 63 ft. 5 in.; height, 16 ft. 3 in.; wing area, 514·7 sq. ft.

HAWKER SIDDELEY HARRIER G.R. MK.1

Country of Origin: United Kingdom.
Type: Single-seat V/STOL strike and reconnaissance fighter.
Power Plant: One Rolls-Royce Bristol Pegasus 101 vectored-thrust turbofan rated at 19,200 lb.s.t.
Performance: (Estimated) Max. speed, 680–720 m.p.h. (Mach 0·9–0·95) at 1,000 ft., (with typical external ordnance load), 640–660 m.p.h. (Mach 0·85–0·87) at 1,000 ft.; tactical radius (hi-lo-hi mission), 350 mls.; ferry range (with two 330 Imp. gal. ferry tanks), 2,300 mls.; time to 10,000 ft., 40 sec.
Weights: (Estimated) Empty equipped, 12,000 lb.; max. loaded (VTOL), 16,000 lb., (STOL), 23,000 lb.
Armament: Maximum external load of 5,000 lb. Typical combat load (short-range interdiction) comprises two 30-mm. Aden cannon pods, two 1,000-lb. and two 750-lb. bombs, or two 30-mm. cannon and four MATRA 116 launchers for 68-mm. SNEB missiles.
Status: In production. First of six pre-production aircraft flown August 31, 1966, and first of initial quantity of 77 Harrier G.R. Mk. 1s for R.A.F. flown December 28, 1967. First two-seat T. Mk. 2 flown April 24 and second July 14, 1969, and delivery of 13 production examples to commence July 1970.
Notes: Capable of Mach 1·25 in dive. First of four R.A.F. Harrier G.R. Mk. 1 squadrons (No. 1 Sqdn.) scheduled to achieve full operational status early 1970. Single-seat Harrier Mk. 50 (P.1176 Super Harrier) and two-seat Harrier Mk. 51 to have 21,500 lb.s.t. Pegasus 11 engine.

HAWKER SIDDELEY HARRIER G.R. MK. 1

Dimensions: Span, 25 ft. 3 in.; length, 46 ft. 4 in.; height, 10 ft. 9 in.; wing area, 201 sq. ft.

HAWKER SIDDELEY NIMROD M.R. MK. 1

Country of Origin: United Kingdom.
Type: Long-range maritime patrol aircraft.
Power Plants: Four Rolls-Royce Spey Mk. 250 turbofans each rated at (approx.) 11,500 lb.s.t.
Performance: (Estimated) Max. cruise, 500–530 m.p.h. at 31,000–33,000 ft.; long-range cruise, 450–460 m.p.h. at 30,000–35,000 ft.; min. search speed, 210 m.p.h.; loiter endurance (on two engines), 12–14 hr.
Weights: Max. loaded, 160,000–170,000 lb.
Armament: Homing torpedoes, depth bombs, etc. in ventral weapons bay, and ASMs on wing pylons.
Accommodation: Normal crew complement of 11 members and (for emergency operation in transport role) 45 troops in rear pressure cabin.
Status: First prototype flown May 23, 1967, and second July 31, 1967. First of 38 production aircraft flown June 28, 1968, and first handed over to R.A.F. Strike Command on October 2, 1969.
Notes: The Nimrod employs the basic structure of the Comet 4C transport, and will become operational in June 1970 with No. 201 Sqdn.

HAWKER SIDDELEY NIMROD M.R. MK. 1

Dimensions: Span, 114 ft. 10 in.; length, 126 ft. 9 in.; height, 29 ft. 8½ in.; wing area, 2,121 sq. ft.

HAWKER SIDDELEY TRIDENT 3B

Country of Origin: United Kingdom.
Type: Short-haul commercial transport.
Power Plants: Three Rolls-Royce Spey RB.163-25 Mk. 512-5W turbofans each rated at 11,930 lb.s.t., and one Rolls-Royce RB.162 turbojet rated at 5,250 lb.s.t.
Performance: (Estimated at 150,000 lb.) Max. cruise, 601 m.p.h. at 28,300 ft.; econ. cruise, 533 m.p.h. at 29,000–33,000 ft.; range (max. fuel, 23,500-lb. payload, and normal reserves and allowances), 1,658 mls., (max. payload—31,900 lb. for 152-seat arrangement), 1,094 mls.
Weights: Operational empty (128 seats), 83,473 lb., (152 seats), 83,104 lb.; max. take-off, 150,000 lb.
Accommodation: Basic flight crew of three and alternative arrangements for 14 first-class and 114 tourist-class passengers, 152 tourist-class passengers, or high-density seating for 164 or 171 passengers.
Status: First Trident 3B flown on December 11, 1969 with first delivery (to B.E.A.) scheduled for early 1971 with six in service by April of that year. Twenty-six ordered by B.E.A. which also has option on 10 additional aircraft.
Notes: The Trident 3B is a high-capacity short-haul development of the Trident 1E with a stretched fuselage (16 ft. 5 in.). Similar wing to Trident 2E (see 1969 edition) but area and flap span increased, and auxiliary turbojet installed in tail to improve take-off performance.

HAWKER SIDDELEY TRIDENT 3B

Dimensions: Span, 98 ft. 0 in.; length, 131 ft. 2 in.; height, 28 ft. 3 in.; wing area, 1,493 sq. ft.

HAWKER SIDDELEY VULCAN B. MK. 2

Country of Origin: United Kingdom.
Type: Long-range medium bomber.
Power Plants: Four Bristol Siddeley Olympus B.Ol.21
Mk. 301 turbojets each rated at 20,000 lb.s.t.
Performance: (Estimated) Max. speed, 645 m.p.h. at
40,000–45,000 ft. (Mach 0·98); max. cruise, 620 m.p.h.
at 45,000 ft. (Mach 0·94); max. cruise altitude, 55,000
ft.; tactical radius (for hi-lo-lo-hi sortie profile), 1,700
mls., (at 40,000–55,000 ft.), 2,300 mls.; max. range,
4,750 mls.
Weights: Loaded, 180,000–200,000 lb.
Armament: Twenty-one 1,000-lb general-purpose
bombs, or free-fall nuclear weapons.
Status: Production completed. First B. Mk. 2 flown
August 19, 1958, deliveries to R.A.F. Bomber Command (now incorporated in Strike Command) commencing July 1960. Production completed 1964.
Notes: Equipping the seven bomber squadrons of No.
1 Group R.A.F. Strike Command, the Vulcan B. Mk.
2 was originally conceived for the high-altitude role
but its mission capability has been extended to
include low-level penetration, and it is expected to
remain in first-line service until the mid-seventies,
although since 1969 its primary role has been tactical,
and the Blue Steel stand-off missile formerly carried
by three of the Vulcan squadrons has been phased out
of service. At the disposal of N.A.T.O. for long-range
tactical strike missions with conventional weapons, the
Vulcan squadrons have a declining responsibility as the
R.A.F.'s main strike element. The Vulcan B. Mk. 2
was preceded by 45 examples of the B. Mk. 1.

HAWKER SIDDELEY VULCAN B. MK. 2

Dimensions: Span, 111 ft. 0 in.; length, 99 ft. 11 in.;
height, 27 ft. 2 in.; wing area, 3,964 sq. ft.

ILYUSHIN IL-62 (CLASSIC)

Country of Origin: U.S.S.R.

Type: Long-range commercial transport.

Power Plants: Four Kuznetsov NK-8-4 turbofans each rated at 23,150 lb.s.t.

Performance: Max. cruise, 560 m.p.h. at 29,500 ft., long-range cruise, 516 m.p.h. at 36,090 ft.; range with max. fuel and 22,046-lb. payload plus one hour's reserves, 6,103 mls., with max. payload—50,706 lb., 4,928 mls.; initial climb (at 340,610 lb.), 3,937 ft./min., (at 352,740 lb.), 3,543 ft./min.; time to 32,810 ft. (at 352,740 lb.), 21 min.; normal operational altitude, 36,090 ft.

Weights: Empty operational, 153,000 lb.; max. take-off, 357,000 lb.

Accommodation: Flight crew of five and arrangements for 186 passengers in high-density layout, 168 passengers in tourist-class layout, and 115 passengers in first-class layout.

Status: In production. First of two prototypes flown January 1963, production being initiated late in 1965.

Notes: The Il-62 entered service with Aeroflot in 1967, the inaugural Moscow–Montreal Il-62 service being operated on September 15, 1967. The Kuznetsov NK-8-3 turbofans of the initial production version have been supplanted by the improved NK-8-4 which, in turn, are expected to give place to 25,353 lb.s.t. Soloviev D-30K turbofans during 1970–71. A 204-passenger stretched version, the Il-62M, is scheduled for Aeroflot service from 1971, this having additional fuselage sections increasing overall length by 21 ft. 4 in.

ILYUSHIN IL-62 (CLASSIC)

Dimensions: Span, 142 ft. 0¾ in.; length, 174 ft. 2½ in.; height, 40 ft. 8 in.; wing area, 3,037·57 sq. ft.

LET L 410 TURBOLET

Country of Origin: Czechoslovakia.

Type: Light utility transport and feederliner.

Power Plants: Two Pratt & Whitney PT6A-27 turbo-props each rated at 715 e.s.h.p.

Performance: Max. cruise, 229 m.p.h. at 9,840 ft.; econ. cruise (80% max. cruise power), 209 m.p.h. at 9,840 ft.; range (freighter with 4,085-lb. payload), 115 mls., (3,355-lb. payload), 370 mls.; max. range (45 min. reserves), 708 mls.; initial climb, 1,595 ft./min.; service ceil., 25,490 ft.

Weights: Empty equipped, 6,418 lb.; max. take-off, 11,244 lb.

Accommodation: Basic flight crew of two and alternative main cabin arrangements for 12, 15, 19 and 20 passengers, or executive configuration with accommodation for eight passengers.

Status: First of three prototypes flown April 16, 1969. Production of initial batch of 20 to commence 1970 with deliveries in 1971.

Notes: First prototype of Turbolet (illustrated) differs from the initial production model described by the specification in having a shorter fuselage (40 ft. 10½ in.). The Turbolet is to be offered in the West with PT6A-27 engines and in the East with the indigenous M 601 turboprop which is expected to be available from late 1972 at a rating of 730 e.s.h.p. Aeromedical and trainer versions are proposed, and it is anticipated that 40 will be ordered by the Czech Air Force.

128

LET L 410 TURBOLET

Dimensions: Span, 56 ft. 1¼ in.; length, 44 ft. 7½ in.;
height, 18 ft. 0½ in.; wing area, 349·827 sq. ft.

LET Z 37 ČMELÁK

Country of Origin: Czechoslovakia.

Type: Light agricultural monoplane.

Power Plant: One M 462 RF nine-cylinder radial engine rated at 315 h.p.

Performance: Normal cruise, 106 m.p.h. at 4,920 ft.; operating speed, 75 m.p.h.; range (as freighter with reserves for one hour's flying plus 10%), 398 mls.; initial climb (at 4,080 lb.), 728 ft./min.

Weights: Empty (without agricultural equipment), 2,171 lb.; max. take-off, 4,080 lb.

Accommodation: Pilot in enclosed cockpit forward of hopper/chemical tank which has capacity of 1,320 lb. or 154 Imp. gal. Provision for auxiliary seat behind hopper/tank for mechanic or loader.

Status: First prototype flown June 29, 1963, with first production deliveries following in 1964.

Notes: In continuous production for six years, the Čmelák (Bumble Bee) is suitable for use as a light utility freighter as well as for agricultural spraying and dusting, and variants of the basic aircraft include an experimental model with a 300 h.p. Continental IO-520-D six-cylinder horizontally-opposed engine which commenced flight testing in 1968, and the Z 37-2 Sparka two-seat conversion trainer (illustrated on opposite page) which commenced flight testing in 1969. The Z 37-2 has no chemical hopper or tank, its space being occupied by a second cockpit with full dual controls. The Z 37-2 is structurally and dimensionally similar to the standard Čmelák.

130

LET Z 37-2 SPARKA

Dimensions: Span, 40 ft. 1 in.; length, 28 ft. 0¾ in.; height, 9 ft. 6 in.; wing area, 256·2 sq. ft.

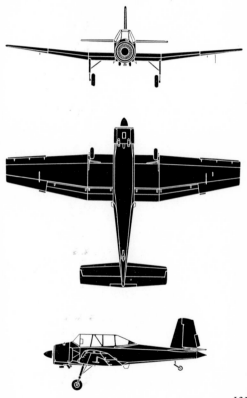

LING-TEMCO-VOUGHT A7D CORSAIR II

Country of Origin: U.S.A.

Type: Single-seat tactical strike fighter.

Power Plant: One Allison TF41-A-1 (Rolls-Royce RB.168-62 Spey) turbofan rated at 14,250 lb.s.t.

Performance: Max. speed (no external stores and 60% fuel), 699 m.p.h. (Mach 0·92) at sea level, (with 12 250-lb. Mk. 81SE bombs), 633 m.p.h., (with 10 750-lb. M 117 bombs), 604 m.p.h.; tactical radius (internal fuel and one hour on station for hi-lo-hi mission with 12 Mk. 81SE bombs), 512 mls. at average cruise of 532 m.p.h., (with 10 M 117 bombs), 390 mls. at average cruise of 509 m.p.h.; ferry range (internal fuel), 2,775 mls., (with four 250 Imp. gal. drop tanks), 3,880 mls.; initial climb (no external stores and 60% fuel), 13,550 ft./min.

Weights: Empty equipped, 19,276 lb.; loaded (clean), 30,000 lb.; max. overload, 43,720 lb.

Armament: One 20-mm. M-61A-1 rotary cannon with 1,000 rounds, plus max. ordnance load (for short-range interdiction) of 15,000 lb. on eight stations.

Status: In production. First A-7D (with TF30-P-6) flown April 6, 1968. First A-7D (with TF41-A-1) flown September 26, 1968. Deliveries to U.S.A.F. commenced December 23, 1968, with first Tactical Air Command wing (54th T.F.W.) attaining operational status mid-1971.

Notes: The A-7D is a land-based derivative of the U.S. Navy's A-7 (see 1968 edition) with new engine, increased armour, revised avionics, etc. The U.S. Navy's 69th and subsequent A-7Es has a 15,000 lb.s.t. TF41-A-2 turbofan and similar avionics to the A-7D.

132

LING-TEMCO-VOUGHT A-7D CORSAIR II

Dimensions: Span, 38 ft. 8¾ in.; length, 46 ft. 1½ in.;
height, 16 ft. 2 in.; wing area, 375 sq. ft.

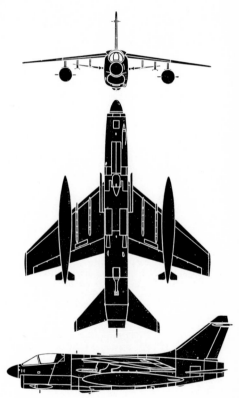

LOCKHEED L-1011 TRISTAR

Country of Origin: U.S.A.

Type: Short- to medium-haul commercial transport.

Power Plants: Three Rolls-Royce RB.211-22 turbofans each rated at 40,600 lb.s.t.

Performance: Max. cruise (with 280 passengers plus 5,000 lb. freight), 570 m.p.h. at 32,500 ft. (Mach 0·85); range cruise, 530 m.p.h. at 35,000 ft. (Mach 0·8); range (with 56,200-lb. payload), 3,270 mls. at Mach 0·85, (with max. payload—84,596 lb.), 2,250 mls. at Mach 0·8; max. operating altitude, 42,000 ft.

Weights: Empty, 208,553 lb.; operational empty, 223,904 lb.; max. take-off, 409,000 lb.

Accommodation: Basic flight crew of three–four and 279 coach-class passengers in eight-abreast seating, or 330 passengers in nine-abreast seating.

Status: First TriStar scheduled to be rolled out in September 1970 with initial flight following before end of year. First deliveries (to Eastern) late 1971, and planned production rate of 10 per month by early 1973. TriStar orders placed by December 1969 totalled 181.

Notes: The initial L-1011-1 version of the TriStar described and illustrated is expected to be joined in the mid 'seventies by an extended-range intercontinental version, the L-1011-8.4, with 52,500 lb.s.t. RB.211-56 turbofans (expected to be available in 1973) or 55,000 lb.s.t. RB.211-57 turbofans (available late 1974). The fuselage of the L-1011-8.4 version of the TriStar will be lengthened by 40 in., providing a maximum capacity of 338 passengers, the wing will be enlarged by some 20%, and with -56 engines max. take-off weight will be 575,000 lb.

134

LOCKHEED L-1011 TRISTAR

Dimensions: Span, 155 ft. 4 in.; length, 177 ft. 8 in.; height, 55 ft. 4 in.; wing area, 3,456 sq. ft.

LOCKHEED C-5A GALAXY

Country of Origin: U.S.A.

Type: Long-range military strategic transport.

Power Plants: Four General Electric TF39-GE-1 turbofans each rated at 41,000 lb.s.t.

Performance: (Estimated) Max. cruise, 540 m.p.h.; long-range cruise, 506 m.p.h.; range at long-range cruise, (with 265,000-lb. payload), 3,110 mls., (with 220,000-lb. payload), 3,510 mls., (with 100,000-lb. payload), 6,680 mls.; initial climb (at 712,000 lb.), 2,150 ft./min.

Weights: Operational empty, 323,904 lb.; normal loaded, 728,000 lb.; max. overload, 769,000 lb.

Accommodation: Basic flight crew of six plus relief crew of six, courier seating for eight plus 75 troops in compartment above cargo hold. Typical loads include two 4·46-ton trucks and ammunition trailers; two Iroquois helicopters; one M41 or M551 tank; two Minuteman missiles mounted on transporters.

Status: First of eight test and evaluation aircraft flown June 30, 1968, and remainder flown by end of 1969. Current order for 81 C-5As with last scheduled for completion in January 1972.

Notes: Current plans call for U.S.A.F. Military Airlift Command to operate four squadrons of 16 Galaxies, with first squadron to be formed at Charleston A.F.B. during 1970. Small number of C-5As expected to be ordered for the R.A.F.

LOCKHEED C-5A GALAXY

Dimensions: Span, 222 ft. 7¼ in.; length, 245 ft. 10¾ in.; height, 65 ft. 1¼ in.; wing area, 6,200 sq. ft.

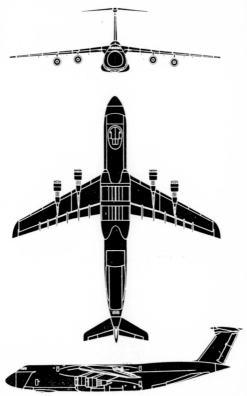

LOCKHEED (C-130K) HERCULES C. MK. 1

Country of Origin: U.S.A.

Type: Medium- to long-range combat transport.

Power Plants: Four Allison T56-A-15 turboprops each rated at 4,910 e.s.h.p. (but limited to 4,500 e.s.h.p.).

Performance: (At 155,000 lb.) Max. speed, 384 m.p.h.; max. cruise, 375 m.p.h.; econ. cruise, 340 m.p.h.; max. payload range (with 5% reserves and allowance for 30 min. at sea level), 2,450 mls.; max. fuel range (similar reserves and allowances), 4,770 mls.; initial climb, 1,900 ft./min.; service ceil. (at 130,000 lb.), 33,000 ft.

Weights: Empty equipped, 72,367 lb.; normal max. loaded, 155,000 lb.; max. overload, 175,000 lb.

Accommodation: Normal flight crew of four and max. of 92 troops, 64 paratroops, or 74 casualty stretchers.

Status: First C-130K flown October 19, 1966, and contracts for 66 completed 1968. The 1,000th Hercules (an HC-130H for U.S. Coast Guard) delivered April 26, 1968, and approx. 1,070 Hercules of all types completed by beginning of 1970 when production was continuing.

Notes: The Hercules C. Mk. 1 (C-130K) of the R.A.F. is essentially similar to the C-130E apart from equipment and power plants, the C-130E having 4,050 e.s.h.p. T56-A-7As. Hercules variants include AC-130A gunship, the EC-130E, G and Q with special electronics, and the HC-130E, H, P and N rescue and recovery aircraft.

LOCKHEED (C-130K) HERCULES C. MK. 1

Dimensions: Span, 132 ft. 7¼ in.; length, 99 ft. 6 in.;
height, 38 ft. 2½ in.; wing area, 1,745 sq. ft.

LOCKHEED C-141A STARLIFTER

Country of Origin: U.S.A.
Type: Long-range military strategic transport.
Power Plants: Four Pratt & Whitney TF33-P-7 turbofans each rated at 21,000 lb.s.t.
Performance: Max. speed, 570 m.p.h.; max. cruise, 562 m.p.h.; long-range cruise, 506 m.p.h.; initial climb, 3,200 ft./min.; service ceil. (at 250,000 lb.), 40,000 ft.; range (with 70,847-lb. payload), 3,973 mls., (with max. fuel and 30,877-lb. payload), 6,045 mls.; ferry, 6,822 mls.
Weights: Empty equipped, 133,773 lb.; max. loaded, 316,100 lb.
Accommodation: Normal flight crew of four, and a maximum of 154 troops, 123 paratroops, or 80 casualty stretchers and eight medical attendants. Up to 5,283 cu. ft. of freight may be loaded on 10 pallets.
Status: First test and evaluation aircraft flown December 17, 1963, and first delivery to U.S.A.F. Military Airlift Command on October 20, 1964, the 289th and last being delivered on February 28, 1968.
Notes: The StarLifter equips 14 Military Airlift Command squadrons, the last of which, the 30th Military Airlift Squadron, began re-equipping in August 1967. The StarLifter is the flying component of Logistics Support System 476L which is intended to provide global range airlift for the U.S.A.F.'s Military Airlift Command, this including the Strategic Army Corps and the Composite Air Strike Forces of the Tactical Air Command.

LOCKHEED C-141A STARLIFTER

Dimensions: Span, 160 ft. 1 in.; length, 145 ft. 0 in., height, 39 ft. 4 in.; wing area, 3,228 sq. ft.

LOCKHEED F-104S STARFIGHTER

Country of Origin: U.S.A.

Type: Single-seat interceptor and strike fighter.

Power Plant: One General Electric J79-GE-19 turbojet rated at 11,870 lb.s.t. and 17,900 lb.s.t. with afterburning.

Performance: Max. speed, 1,450 m.p.h. at 40,000 ft. (Mach 2·2), 915 m.p.h. at 1,000 ft. (Mach 1·2); max. cruise, 610 m.p.h. at 36,000 ft. (Mach 0·92); initial climb, 50,000+ ft./min.; combat ceil., 57,000 ft.; tactical radius (with two 162 Imp. gal./200 U.S. gal. and two 100 Imp. gal./120 U.S. gal. drop tanks), 740–775 mls.; ferry range, 2,200 mls.

Weights: Empty, 14,573 lb.; loaded (clean), 21,307 lb.; max. loaded, 31,000 lb.

Armament: One 20-mm. M-61 Vulcan rotary cannon and two AIM-7 Sparrow III semi-active radar homing and two AIM-9 Sidewinder infra-red homing AAMs.

Status: In production. First of two F-104S prototypes flown December 1966. Production of 165 in Italy with orders placed for 82 by beginning of 1970, options being held on the remaining 83. First Fiat-built F-104S flown on December 30, 1968, and production rate of four per month at beginning of 1970.

Notes: The F-104S is a derivative of the F-104G (see 1966 edition) intended primarily for the all-weather intercept role. Two prototypes have been modified by the parent company from Italian-manufactured F-104G airframes, and licence manufacture is being undertaken for the Italian Air Force by Fiat. The F-104S is intended to take over the entire *Aeronautica Militare* manned fighter intercept commitment by 1972.

LOCKHEED F-104S STARFIGHTER

Dimensions: Span, 21 ft. 11 in.; length, 54 ft. 9 in.;
height, 13 ft. 6 in.; wing area, 196·1 sq. ft.

LOCKHEED P-3C ORION

Country of Origin: U.S.A.

Type: Long-range maritime patrol aircraft.

Power Plants: Four Allison T56-A-14W turboprops each rated at 4,910 e.s.h.p. (4,591 s.h.p.).

Performance: (At 105,000 lb.) Max. speed, 476 m.p.h. at 15,000 ft.; normal cruise, 397 m.p.h. at 25,000 ft.; initial climb, 3,270 ft./min.: loiter endurance (four engines) at 1,500 ft., 12·9 hr., (two engines), 17 hr.; max. mission radius (3 hr. on station at 1,500 ft.), 2,533 mls.

Weights: Empty, 61,000 lb.; max. loaded, 133,500 lb.; max. overload, 142,000 lb.

Accommodation: Normal crew of 10 comprising pilot, co-pilot, flight engineer, navigator-radioman, tactical co-ordinator, three sensor operators and two observers, and for emergency troop carrier role up to 50 combat troops and 4,000 lb. of equipment.

Armament: Weapons bay can accommodate two Mk. 101 nuclear depth bombs and four Mk. 43, 44 or 46 torpedoes, or eight Mk. 54 bombs. All 10 external pylons can carry torpedoes, mines or rockets, maximum external stores load being 13,713 lb.

Status: YP-3C prototype (illustrated) flown on October 8, 1968, and first deliveries of P-3C to U.S. Navy early 1969.

Notes: One hundred and fifty-seven examples of the initial production version of the Orion, the P-3A, delivered to U.S. Navy, and followed by P-3B (see 1969 edition) also delivered to Norway (5), New Zealand (5), and Australia (10). Extensively revised P-3C with A-New integrated airborne ASW system entered service with VP-56 mid-1969.

144

LOCKHEED P-3C ORION

Dimensions: Span, 99 ft. 8 in.; length, 116 ft. 10 in.; height, 33 ft. 8½ in.; wing area, 1,300 sq. ft.

K

McDONNELL DOUGLAS A-4F SKYHAWK

Country of Origin: U.S.A.

Type: Single-seat shipboard attack bomber.

Power Plant: One Pratt & Whitney J52-P-8A turbojet rated at 9,300 lb.s.t.

Performance: Max. speed (without external stores), 675 m.p.h. at sea level (Mach 0·88), 612 m.p.h. at 35,000 ft. (Mach 0·92); max. speed in high drag configuration, 610 m.p.h. at sea level (Mach 0·8), 575 m.p.h. at 30,000 ft. (Mach 0·85); combat radius (with 4,000 lb. external stores), 380 mls.; ferry range (max. fuel), 2,440 mls.; service ceil. (clean), 47,900 ft.

Weights: Empty, 9,940 lb.; loaded (clean), 16,300 lb.; max. loaded, 27,420 lb.

Armament: Two 20-mm. Mk. 12 cannon with 100 r.p.g. plus a maximum of 8,200 lb. of stores for shipboard and 11,800 lb. for shore-based operation.

Status: First A-4F flown August 31, 1966. Deliveries of 150 initiated June 20, 1967, preceded by 139 two-seat TA-4Fs.

Notes: A-4F differs from A-4E in having more powerful engine, steerable nosewheel, zero-zero escape system, avionics compartment aft of cockpit and wing, lift spoilers. Tandem two-seat training version, the TA-4F, followed by TA-4J with 8,500 lb.s.t. J52-P-6 and relocated and simplified equipment. Export equivalents comprise A-4G (8) and TA-4G for Australian Navy; A-4H (65) and TA-4H (8) for Israel, and A-4K (10) and TA-4K (4) for R.N.Z.A.F. Current single-seat production model for U.S. Navy is A-4M with J52-P-400.

146

McDONNELL DOUGLAS A-4F SKYHAWK

Dimension: Span, 27 ft. 6 in.; length, 42 ft. 10¾ in.; height, 15 ft. 2 in.; wing area, 260 sq. ft.

McDONNELL DOUGLAS DC-8
SUPER 60 SERIES

Country of Origin: U.S.A.

Type: Long-range commercial transport.

Power Plants: Four Pratt & Whitney JT3D-3B turbofans each rated at 18,000 lb.s.t., or (Super 63) JT3D-7 turbofans each rated at 19,000 lb.s.t.

Performance: (Variant indicated in parentheses) Max. cruise at 220,000 lb., (61) 580 m.p.h., (62) 586 m.p.h., (63) 583 m.p.h.; initial climb at max. loaded weight, (61) 2,270 ft./min., (62) 2,240 ft./min., (63) 2,165 ft./min.; max. range without payload, (61) 7,370 mls., (62) 8,780 mls., (63) 8,100 mls.

Weights: Operational empty, (61) 150,298 lb., (62) 143,653 lb., (63) 156,755 lb.; max. take-off, (61) 325,000 lb., (62) 335,000 lb., (63) 350,000 lb.

Accommodation: The maximum economy class passenger accommodation of the Super 60 series is as follows. (61) 251, (62) 189, (63) 251 plus 14,000 lb. freight. The space-limited payloads of the freighter equivalents are : (61F) 91,250 lb., (62F) 96,754 lb., (63F) 91,614 lb.

Status: First DC-8-61 flown March 14, 1966, first DC-8-62 flown August 29, 1966, and first DC-8-63 flown April 10, 1967. Approx. 510 DC-8s of all versions delivered by beginning of 1970.

Notes: Stretched derivatives of DC-8-50 (see 1966 edition). DC-8-61 and -61F feature 36·9-ft. increase in fuselage length. DC-8-62 and -62F have shorter fuselage, 3-ft. wingtip extensions, new engine pylons suspending the engines 40 in. forward of previous installations, and redesigned long-duct engine pods offering reduced drag. The DC-8-63 (illustrated) and -63F have similar fuselage to -61 coupled with aerodynamic refinements of -62.

148

McDONNELL DOUGLAS DC-8 SUPER 60 SERIES

Dimensions: Span (61), 142 ft. 4¾ in., (62 and 63) 148 ft. 4¾ in.; length (61 and 63), 187 ft. 4¾ in., (62) 157 ft. 4¾ in.; height, 42 ft. 3½ in.; wing area (61), 2,884 sq. ft., (62 and 63) 2,926·8 sq. ft.

McDONNELL DOUGLAS DC-9 SERIES 20

Country of Origin: U.S.A.

Type: Short- to medium-range commercial transport.

Power Plants: Two Pratt & Whitney JT8D-9 turbofans each rated at 14,500 lb.s.t.

Performance: Max. cruise, 560 m.p.h. at 25,000 ft.; range (with 50 passengers and reserves for 230 miles and 60 min. holding at 10,000 ft.), 1,397 mls. at 25,000 ft., (long-range cruise), 1,840 mls. at 30,000 ft.

Weights: Empty, 51,661 lb.; max. take-off, 98,000 lb.

Accommodation: Flight crew of two–three, and maximum of 90 tourist-class passengers in five-abreast seating.

Status: In production. First DC-9-20 flown on September 18, 1968, and first deliveries (to S.A.S.) late same year. More than 550 DC-9s of all versions had been completed by the beginning of 1970.

Notes: Claimed to possess the highest lift coefficient of any commercial transport, and capable of operating from airfields previously accessible only to airscrew-driven aircraft, the DC-9-20 combines the short DC-9-10 (see 1966 edition) fuselage with the wing developed for the larger DC-9-30 (see 1968 edition). Alternative power plants are 15,000 lb.s.t. JT8D-11s with which max. take-off weight is increased to 100,000 lb. A further version with a 21-ft. longer fuselage than that of the DC-9-20 but with similar wings and power plants is the DC-9-40 which was flown for the first time on November 28, 1967. A U.S.A.F. aeromedical evacuation transport derivative of the DC-9-30, the C-5A Nightingale, is described in the 1969 edition.

150

McDONNELL DOUGLAS DC-9 SERIES 20

Dimensions: Span, 93 ft. 3½ in.; length, 104 ft. 4¾ in.; height, 27 ft. 6 in.; wing area, 1,000·7 sq. ft.

McDONNELL DOUGLAS DC-10 SERIES 10

Country of Origin: U.S.A.

Type: Short- to medium-haul commercial transport.

Power Plants: Three General Electric CF6-6 turbofans each rated at 40,000 lb.s.t.

Performance: Max. cruise (80,177-lb. payload—270 passengers), 570 m.p.h. at 32,000 ft. (Mach 0·85); range cruise, 540 m.p.h. at 35,000 ft. (Mach 0·82); range (with 54,000-lb. payload), 3,545 mls. at Mach 0·82.

Weights: Operational empty, 230,323 lb.; max. take-off, 410,000 lb.

Accommodation: Basic flight crew of three–four and maximum of 343 passengers in nine-abreast coach-class seating, or (typical) mixed-class arrangement for 48 first-class and 222 coach-class passengers.

Status: First DC-10 Srs. 10 scheduled to be rolled out during second half of 1970 and flown before end of year. First five to be used for flight development and certification programme, and first deliveries to commence autumn 1971. DC-10 orders placed by December 1969 totalled 89.

Notes: In addition to the Srs. 10, extended-range inter-continental versions of the DC-10 are currently under development for delivery from late 1972, these being the Srs. 20 with 49,800 lb.s.t. Pratt & Whitney JT9D-17 turbofans, and the Srs. 30 with 49,000 lb.s.t. General Electric CF6-50A turbofans. The external dimensions of all three models are similar. An all-cargo or convertible cargo–passenger version is designated DC-10F.

152

McDONNELL DOUGLAS DC-10 SERIES 10

Dimensions: Span, 155 ft. 4 in.; length, 180 ft. 0 in.; height, 58 ft. 1 in.; wing area, 3,550 sq. ft.

McDONNELL DOUGLAS F-4E PHANTOM II

Country of Origin: U.S.A.

Type: Two-seat tactical strike fighter.

Power Plants: Two General Electric J79-GE-17 turbojets each rated at 11,870 lb.s.t. and 17,900 lb.s.t. with afterburning.

Performance: Max. speed in clean condition, 1,498 m.p.h. at 40,000 ft. (Mach 2·27), 910 m.p.h. at sea level (Mach 1·2); initial climb (at 46,297 lb.), 30,000 ft./min.; tactical radius (with four Sparrow III and four Sidewinder AAMs), 140 mls., (plus one 500 Imp. gal. aux. tank), 196 mls., (hi-lo-hi mission with four 1,000-lb. bombs, four AAMs, one 500 and two 308 Imp. gal. tanks), 656 mls., (lo-lo-hi with similar stores), 460 mls.; max. ferry range, 2,300 mls. at 575 m.p.h. cruise at 40,000 ft.

Weights: Empty, 30,425 lb.; loaded (four Sparrow IIIs), 51,810 lb., (max. external fuel, four Sparrows and four Sidewinders), 58,000 lb.; max. overload, 60,630 lb.

Armament: One 20-mm. M-61A1 rotary cannon and (intercept) four or six AIM-7E Sparrow IIIB plus four AIM-9D Sidewinder 1C AAMs, or (attack) up to 16,000 lb. of external stores.

Status: First F-4E flown June 30, 1967. The 3,000th Phantom delivered September 5, 1968 and approx. 4,000 delivered by beginning of 1970.

Notes: The F-4E is current U.S.A.F. production version of the Phantom, a reconnaissance version being the RF-4E. Fifty F-4Es and six RF-4Es in process of delivery to Israel, 88 RF-4Es ordered by Federal Germany, and 104 F-4EJs to be built in Japan.

154

McDONNELL DOUGLAS F-4E PHANTOM II

Dimensions: Span, 38 ft. 4¾ in.; length, 62 ft. 10 in.; height, 16 ft. 3 in.; wing area, 530 sq. ft.

McDONNELL DOUGLAS (F-4M)
PHANTOM F.G.R. MK. 2

Country of Origin: U.S.A.

Type: Two-seat strike and reconnaissance fighter.

Power Plants: Two Rolls-Royce RB.168-25R Spey Mk. 202 turbofans each rated at 12,250 lb.s.t. and 20,515 lb.s.t. with afterburning.

Performance: Max. speed, 1,386 m.p.h. at 40,000 ft. (Mach 2·1), 910 m.p.h. at sea level (Mach 1·2); tactical radius (hi-lo-hi mission with six 1,000-lb. bombs and two 308 Imp. gal. aux. tanks), 550 mls., (lo-lo-hi with similar external stores), 380 mls.; ferry range (max. external fuel), 2,500 mls.

Weights: Approx. empty equipped, 30,000 lb.; approx. loaded (four Sparrow IIIs and two 308 Imp. gal. aux. tanks), 49,000 lb.; max. loaded, 58,000 lb.

Armament: (Intercept) One 20-mm. M-61A1 rotary cannon in SUU 23A centreline pod, four AIM-7E Sparrow IIIB and four AIM-9D Sidewinder 1C AAMs, or (attack), 11 1,000-lb. Mk. 14 bombs, 10 Matra MI55 pods each with 18 SNEB 68-mm. rockets, Martel ASMs, etc.

Status: First of two (YF-4M) prototypes flown February 17, 1967, and deliveries of 118 (F-4M) Phantom F.G.R. Mk. 2s to R.A.F. commenced July 1968.

Notes: Anglicised shore-based equivalent of U.S. Navy's F-4J, the Phantom F.G.R. Mk. 2 equips Nos. 6 and 54 Sqdns. R.A.F. Air Support Command, the essentially similar Phantom F.G. Mk. 1 (F-4K), 48 of which were originally intended for the R.N., serving in the intercept role with No. 43 Sqdn., and with the sole R.N. Phantom combat unit, No. 892 Sqdn.

McDONNELL DOUGLAS (F-4M) PHANTOM
F.G.R. MK. 2

Dimensions: Span, 38 ft. 4¾ in.; length, 57 ft. 11 in.;
height, 16 ft. 3⅛ in.; wing area, 530 sq. ft.

MBB BÖ 209 MONSUN

Country of Origin: Federal Germany.
Type: Light cabin monoplane.
Power Plant: (Bö 209A) One Lycoming O-235-C2A four-cylinder horizontally-opposed engine rated at 115 h.p., or (Bö 209B) O-320-E2A four-cylinder horizontally-opposed engine rated at 150 h.p.
Performance: (Specification related to Bö 209A with figures in parentheses applying to the Bö 209B) Max. speed, 153 (168) m.p.h. at sea level; cruise at 75% power, 140 (155) m.p.h.; max. range (65% power and no reserves), 745 (620) mls. at 135 (144) m.p.h.; initial climb, 785 (1,045) ft./min.; service ceil., 14,775 (16,400) ft.
Weights: Empty, 992 (1,045) lb.; max. take-off, 1,653 (1,807) lb.
Accommodation: Side-by-side seats for pilot and one passenger beneath aft-sliding canopy.
Status: Prototype flown (as MHK-101) on December 22, 1967, and first production aircraft on May 28, 1969.
Notes: The Monsun (Monsoon), which is being manufactured by the Bölkow-Apparatebau Division of the Messerschmitt-Bölkow-Blohm (MBB) group, is unusual in having fixed main undercarriage members and a *retractable* nosewheel, this feature being intended to facilitate towing along roads, the wings being folded back along the fuselage sides after the removal of six bolts.

158

MBB BÖ 209 MONSUN

Dimensions: Span, 27 ft. 6¾ in.; length, 21 ft. 0 in.; height, 7 ft. 2½ in.; wing area, 110 sq. ft.

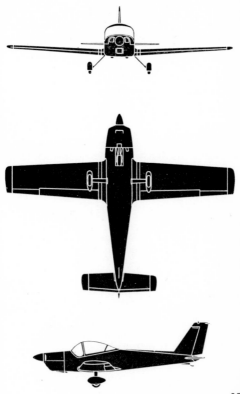

MBB (HFB 320) HANSA JET

Country of Origin: Federal Germany.

Type: Light business executive transport, feederliner and airline crew trainer.

Power Plants: Two General Electric CJ610-5 turbojets each rated at 2,950 lb.s.t. or CJ610-9 turbojets each rated at 3,100 lb.s.t.

Performance: (At 16,530 lb. with CJ610-5 engines) Max. cruise, 513 m.p.h. at 25,000 ft.; econ. cruise, 420 m.p.h. at 35,000 ft.; range (800-lb. payload—four passengers and baggage), 1,500 mls.; initial climb, 4,250 ft./min.; service ceil. (at 17,640 lb.), 37,500 ft.

Weights: Basic operational (including two pilots), 12,125 lb.; max. take-off, 20,280 lb.

Accommodation: Basic flight crew of two and standard configurations for seven, 11 or 15 passengers.

Status: First of two prototypes flown on April 21, 1964, and first production example flown on February 2, 1966. Twenty-four sold by November 1969.

Notes: First 15 Hansa Jets delivered with 2,850 lb.s.t. CJ610-1 turbojets, the uprated CJ610-5 being introduced December 1968 with the CJ610-9 being standardised for 1970 production aircraft. Six delivered to the *Luftwaffe* and three to the *Rijksluchtvaartschool* in Holland, the latter for pilot training. Manufactured by the Hamburger Flugzeugbau, a component of the Messerschmitt-Bölkow-Blohm (MBB) group, the HFB 320 Hansa Jet is being further developed as the HFB 330 Hansa Fanjet which will fly in 1971 with ATF3 turbofans and stretched fuselage (56 ft. 9 in.).

MBB (HFB 320) HANSA JET

Dimensions: Span, 47 ft. 6 in.; length, 54 ft. 6 in.;
height, 16 ft. 2 in.; wing area, 324·4 sq. ft.

MFI-15A

Country of Origin: Sweden.

Type: Side-by-side two-seat primary trainer.

Power Plant: One Lycoming IO-320-B20 four-cylinder horizontally-opposed engine rated at 160 h.p.

Performance: Max. speed (at max. loaded weight), 155 m.p.h.; normal cruise, 137 m.p.h.; range, 470 mls.; time to 6,000 ft., 10 min.

Weights: Max. take-off, 1,907 lb.

Status: Prototype MFI-15A flown for the first time on July 11, 1969. Production status uncertain at time of closing for press.

Notes: An enlarged development of the MFI-9 two-seat light aircraft (of which more than 70 have been built in Sweden and some 200 under licence in Germany as the Bö 208 Junior), the MFI-15 was designed primarily to meet Swedish armed forces' requirements for a primary trainer (Air Force) and a light air observation post (Army). The MFI-15A was proposed to meet the former requirement and the MFI-15B to meet the latter, the "B" model having a tailwheel undercarriage. The Air Force primary trainer requirement is being fulfilled by the Beagle Bulldog, but a Swedish Army decision concerning its choice of a light AOP aircraft had not been announced at the time of closing for press. The luggage compartment may be used for a third seat.

MFI-15A

Dimensions: Span, 28 ft. 6½ in.; length, 22 ft. 1¾ in.; height, 8 ft. 6⅓ in.

MIKOYAN MIG-21PF (FISHBED-F)

Country of Origin: U.S.S.R.

Type: Single-seat all-weather interceptor fighter.

Power Plant: One Tumansky R.37F turbojet rated at approx. 10,000 lb.s.t. and 13,200 lb.s.t. with afterburning.

Performance: Max. speed (without external stores), 1,450 m.p.h. at 36,000–40,000 ft. (Mach 2·2), (with two Atoll AAMs or UV-16-57 rocket pods), 1,320 m.p.h. (Mach 2·0); subsonic cruise tactical radius (without external fuel), 400 mls.; time to 40,000 ft., 4·5 min.

Weights: (Estimated) loaded (with one 132 Imp. gal. centreline drop tank and two Atoll missiles), 17,700 lb.; max. loaded, 19,500 lb.

Armament: Two Atoll AAMs or two UV-16-57 pods each housing 16 55-mm. rockets.

Status: In production. Licence manufacture undertaken in Czechoslovakia and India (latter producing MiG-21FL).

Notes: In its latest form, the MiG-21PF embodies a number of modifications (illustrated by the drawing on the opposite page), including vertical tail surfaces of increased chord, a repositioned braking chute housing, and a new cockpit canopy with separate quarter lights and hood. The export version of the MiG-21PF, the MiG-21FL, differs from the standard model only in avionic equipment, and the MiG-21F (Fishbed-C) is the standard day interceptor model. A tandem-seat training version of the fighter, the MiG-21UTI (Mongol), was described and illustrated in the 1968 edition.

164

MIKOYAN MIG-21PF (FISHBED-F)

Estimated Dimensions: Span, 25 ft. 0 in.; length, 49 ft. 0 in.; height, 15 ft. 0 in.; wing area, 250 sq. ft.

MIKOYAN MIG-23 (FOXBAT)

Country of Origin: U.S.S.R.

Type: Single-seat interceptor and strike fighter.

Power Plants: Two turbojets each rated at approx. 22,000 lb.s.t. and 33,000 lb.s.t. with afterburning.

Performance: (Estimated) Max. speed (short-period dash), 2,110 m.p.h. at 40,000–50,000 ft. (Mach 3·2), 910 m.p.h. at sea level (Mach 1·2).

Weights: Approx. loaded, 90,000 lb.

Status: In production. Believed flown in prototype form 1963–64 with first service deliveries 1967.

Notes: The Foxbat, designated MiG-23 in service form, has established a number of internationally-recognised records as the Ye-266, the first of these being announced in April 1965 and being a 1,000-km. closed circuit record of 1,441·5 m.p.h. (Mach 2·2) carrying a 4,409-lb. payload, the flight being performed between 69,000 and 72,200 ft. In October 1967, the Ye-266 attained 98,458 ft. with a 4,409-lb. payload and covered a 500-km. closed circuit at an average speed of 1,820·6 m.p.h. (Mach 2·76), and on November 4, 1967 averaged 1,807 m.p.h. over a 1,000-km. circuit. The MiG-23 was expected to attain service status in the strike role during the course of 1969, and in the high-altitude intercept role during 1970–71.

MIKOYAN MIG-23 (FOXBAT)

Estimated Dimensions: Span, 47 ft. 0 in.; length, 85 ft. 0 in.; height, 20 ft. 0 in.

MIKOYAN FLOGGER

Country of Origin: U.S.S.R.

Type: Single-seat tactical strike and reconnaissance fighter.

Power Plant: One turbojet rated at 28,000–30,000 lb.s.t. with afterburning.

Performance: (Estimated) Max. speed, 1,650 m.p.h. at 40,000 ft. (Mach 2·5), 910 m.p.h. at sea level (Mach 1·2).

Weights: Approx. loaded, 40,000–45,000 lb.

Status: Believed experimental. Single prototype demonstrated at Domodedovo July 1967. Current status uncertain. Possible service introduction 1969–1970.

Notes: Appreciably smaller and lighter than the General Dynamics F-111 and approximating more closely to the Dassault Mirage G, the Mikoyan-designed variable-geometry fighter was believed to have attained a relatively early development stage at the time of closing for press. The wing design follows U.S. first generation practice closely in that the hinge points are set well out from the fuselage and large fixed wing-root gloves are provided. The wing reportedly translates from the full-forward low-speed position to the full-aft high-speed position in some four seconds. The rectangular air intakes are noteworthy, and the vertical tail surfaces are augmented at high speeds by a large ventral fin which appears to fold sideways for take-off and landing.

168

MIKOYAN FLOGGER

Estimated Dimensions: Span (minimum sweep), 48 ft.
0 in., (maximum sweep), 24 ft. 0 in.; length (including
probe), 60 ft. 0 in.; height, 15 ft. 0 in.

MITSUBISHI MU-2G

Country of Origin: Japan.
Type: Light business executive and utility transport.
Power Plants: Two Garrett AiResearch TPE331-1-151A turboprops each rated at 705 e.s.h.p.
Performance: (At 9,170 lb.) Max. cruise, 326 m.p.h. at 10,000 ft.; econ. cruise, 300 m.p.h. at 20,000 ft.; max. range (at 10,361 lb.), 1,550 mls. at 23,000 ft.; initial climb, 2,600 ft./min.; service ceil., 27,000 ft.
Weights: Empty equipped, 6,426 lb.; max. take-off, 10,361 lb.
Accommodation: Normal flight crew of two and various cabin arrangements for from six to 12 passengers.
Status: Prototype MU-2G flown January 10, 1969, production deliveries commencing during the following autumn. First prototype of initial model (MU-2A) flown September 14, 1963, and approx. 140 of all versions completed by beginning of 1970.
Notes: The MU-2G is a "stretched" version of the MU-2F (see 1969 edition) with lengthened fuselage and mainwheels retracting into external fairings. Variants of the basic design include the Astazou-powered MU-2A (three built), the MU-2A (initial production model with TPE-331-25As of which 34 built), the MU-2C (unpressurised reconnaissance and liaison model for Ground Self-Defence Force of which nine built), the MU-2D (MU-2B with integral fuel tanks), and MU-2E (search and rescue version for Air Self-Defence Force).

MITSUBISHI MU-2G

Dimensions: Span, 39 ft. 2 in.; length, 39 ft. 5¾ in.; height, 13 ft. 8¼ in.; wing area, 178 sq. ft.

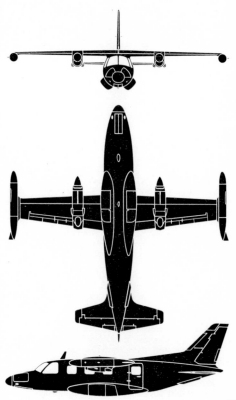

NAMC YS-11T

Country of Origin: Japan.
Type: Anti-submarine warfare trainer.
Power Plants: Two Rolls-Royce Dart 542-10 turbo-props each rated at 2,660 e.h.p. (dry) and 3,060 e.h.p. (wet).
Performance: (YS-11A-200 but generally applicable to the YS-11T) Max. cruise, 291 m.p.h. at 15,000 ft.; econ. cruise, 281 m.p.h. at 20,000 ft.; radius of action (YS-11T), 810 mls. plus 2·5 hr. loiter; initial climb, 1,220 ft./min.; service ceil., 22,900 ft.
Weights: Approx. max. loaded, 54,000 lb.
Accommodation: Basic flight crew of four and ASW avionics to permit simultaneous training of a number of ASW systems operators.
Status: First of four YS-11T trainers for the Maritime Self-Defence Force flown February 1969. The 100th YS-11 completed May 1969, and total of 123 ordered by December 1969.
Notes: The YS-11T is an ASW trainer derivative of the YS-11A-200 short- and medium-haul transport (see 1969 edition), and is the latest of several military versions of the basic design, these including the YS-11M cargo transport based on the YS-11-100 (one delivered) for the Maritime Self-Defence Force, and the YS-11P personnel transport also based on the YS-11-100 (four delivered) for the Air Self-Defence Force. The MSDF also operates a YS-11-400 cargo transport, and the ASDF has three YS-11A-305 mixed personnel/cargo aircraft. The Maritime Safety Board employs one YS-11A-207 for search and rescue tasks.

NAMC YS-11T

Dimensions: Span, 104 ft. 11¾ in.; length, 86 ft. 3½ in.; height, 29 ft. 5¾ in.; wing area, 1,020·4 sq. ft.

NAMC XC-1A

Country of Origin: Japan.
Type: Medium-range military transport.
Power Plants: Two Pratt & Whitney JT8D-9 turbo-fans each rated at 14,500 lb.s.t.
Performance: (Estimated at 85,980 lb.) Max. speed, 507 m.p.h. at 23,200 ft.; max. cruise, 438 m.p.h. at 35,100 ft.; range (with 17,637-lb. payload), 806 mls., (max. fuel and 5,732-lb. payload), 2,073 mls.; initial climb, 3,806 ft./min.; service ceil., 39,370 ft.
Weights: Empty equipped, 50,706 lb.; max. loaded, 85,980 lb.
Accommodation: Basic crew of five and 60 troops, 45 paratroops, or 36 casualty stretchers plus medical attendants. As a cargo transport loads can include a 2½-ton truck, a 105-mm. howitzer, two ¾-ton trucks, or three jeep-type vehicles.
Status: First of two flying prototypes scheduled to commence trials October 1970, and production of the C-1A for the Air Self-Defence Force expected to commence 1971 with first deliveries in 1973.
Notes: The XC-1A has been designed as a successor to the aged Curtiss C-46 in service with the Air Self-Defence Force, the initial requirement being allegedly 50 aircraft. A full-scale mock-up (illustrated above) was completed in March 1968, and detail design was completed in April 1969.

NAMC XC-1A

Dimensions: Span, 101 ft. 8½ in.; length, 95 ft. 1¾ in.; height, 32 ft. 9¾ in.; wing area, 1,291·7 sq. ft.

NORD 262C

Country of Origin: France.
Type: Light short-haul feederliner.
Power Plants: Two Turboméca Bastan VIIA turbo-props each rated at 1,140 s.h.p.
Performance: Max. cruise (80% take-off power), 253 m.p.h. at 15,000 ft.; range (standard fuel, 4,200-lb. payload and full FAA reserves), 795 mls., (29 passengers and baggage), 405 mls., (26 passengers and baggage), 780 mls.
Weights: Max. take-off, 23,370 lb.
Accommodation: Basic flight crew of two and standard seating for 26 passengers in three-abreast rows with two to starboard and one to port. Maximum seating for 29 passengers.
Status: First prototype flown December 24, 1962, and first production model to definitive standards on June 10, 1964. First Nord 262C flown 1968 with deliveries scheduled for early 1970. By the beginning of December 1969 a total of 62 Nord 262s had been delivered against orders for 96 (including 39 for the French armed forces).
Notes: Nord 262D is equivalent Bastan VIIA-powered military version for *Armée de l'Air*, the delivery of 24 having commenced November 1968.

176

Dimensions: Span, 71 ft. 10¼ in.; length, 63 ft. 3 in.; height, 20 ft. 4 in.; wing area, 592 sq. ft.

NORTH AMERICAN ROCKWELL
HAWK COMMANDER

Country of Origin: U.S.A.

Type: Light business executive transport.

Power Plants: Two Garrett AiResearch TPE331-43-BL turboprops each rated at 605 e.s.h.p.

Performance: Max. speed (at 9,000 lb.), 290 m.p.h.; max. cruise (at 9,400 lb.), 278 m.p.h. at 10,000 ft., (at 8,400 lb.), 263 m.p.h. at 21,000 ft.; econ. cruise, 254 m.p.h. at 21,000 ft.; range (45 min. reserves and econ. cruise), 1,062 mls., (with 42·5 Imp. gal. auxiliary fuel), 1,315 mls.; initial climb, 2,007 ft./min.; service ceil., 25,600 ft.

Weights: Empty equipped, 5,515 lb.; max. take-off, 9,400 lb.

Accommodation: Normal flight crew of two and standard seating for six passengers. Optional seating arrangement for up to eight passengers.

Status: Hawk Commander introduced May 1969 as a refinement of the Turbo II Commander, first customer deliveries being effected July 1969. Prototype of original Turbo Commander flew December 31, 1964, first production example following in April 1965.

Notes: Essentially a turboprop-powered equivalent of the piston-engined **Courser Commander** (see 1969 edition).

178

NORTH AMERICAN ROCKWELL
HAWK COMMANDER

Dimensions: Span, 44 ft. 0⅔ in.; length, 42 ft. 11¾ in.;
height, 14 ft. 6 in.; wing area, 242·5 sq. ft.

NORTH AMERICAN ROCKWELL
SHRIKE COMMANDER

Country of Origin: U.S.A.

Type: Light business executive transport.

Power Plants: Two Lycoming IO-540-E1B5 six-cylinder horizontally-opposed engines each rated at 290 h.p.

Performance: (At 6,750 lb.) Max. cruise, 215 m.p.h. at sea level; range cruise (75% power), 203 m.p.h. at 9,000 ft.; range (at 75% power with 45 min. reserves), 750 mls.; max. range (no reserves), 1,078 mls. at 170 m.p.h. at 15,000 ft.; initial climb, 1,340 ft./min.; time to 10,000 ft., 10 min.; service ceil., 19,400 ft.

Weights: Empty equipped, 4,520 lb.; max. take-off, 6,750 lb.

Accommodation: Standard seating for pilot and four passengers in individual seats, but optional arrangements for up to seven persons.

Status: The Shrike Commander is the current production version of the original Aero Commander 500 which has been continuously manufactured in progressively refined versions since 1958. Aerodynamic and power plant changes led, via the Models 500A and 500B, to the Model 500U (the suffix letter indicating that the aircraft now conformed with Part 3 Utility Category Requirements) first offered in 1965, and in 1968 this model received the appellation Shrike Commander, the version described by the specification being introduced in May 1969.

NORTH AMERICAN ROCKWELL
SHRIKE COMMANDER

Dimensions: Span, 49 ft. 0½ in.; length, 36 ft. 7 in.;
height, 14 ft. 6 in.; wing area, 255 sq. ft.

NORTH AMERICAN ROCKWELL
OV-10A BRONCO

Country of Origin: U.S.A.

Type: Tandem two-seat light Counter-insurgency and forward air control aircraft.

Power Plants: Two Garrett-AiResearch T76-G-10/12 turboprops each rated at 715 s.h.p.

Performance: Max. speed (at 9,908 lb.), 279 m.p.h. at sea level, 259 m.p.h. at 20,000 ft.; average cruise, 194 m.p.h.; tactical radius (close support strike mission at 12,500 lb., including 1 hr. loiter in target area, with 146 Imp. gal.), 110 mls., (with 210 Imp. gal.), 215 mls., (with 335 Imp. gal.), 390 mls.; ferry range, 1,428 mls.; initial climb, 2,320 ft./min.

Weights: Empty, 6,969 lb.; normal loaded, 9,908 lb.; max. 14,466 lb.

Armament: Four 7·62-mm. M-60C machine guns with 500 r.p.g., plus ordnance on one 1,200-lb. and four 600-lb. capacity external stations.

Status: First of seven prototypes flown July 16, 1965, and first production August 6, 1967. Deliveries initiated February 23, 1968 against orders for 157 and 114 for the respective services.

Notes: Bronco began operational service in Vietnam with both U.S.A.F. and U.S.M.C. in July 1968. Eighteen to be delivered to Federal Germany as target-tugs from February 1970, 12 having an auxiliary J85 turbojet to boost maximum speed to 375 m.p.h. for high-speed target towing (illustrated opposite).

NORTH AMERICAN ROCKWELL
OV-10B BRONCO

Dimensions: Span, 40 ft. 0 in.; length (including pitot head), 41 ft. 7 in.; height, 15 ft. 1 in.; wing area, 291 sq. ft.

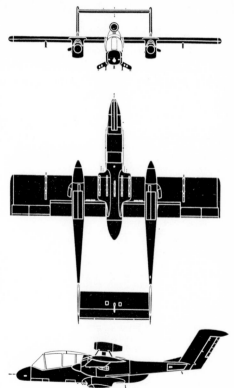

NORTH AMERICAN ROCKWELL RA-5C VIGILANTE

Country of Origin: U.S.A.

Type: Tandem two-seat shipboard strategic reconnaissance and attack bomber.

Power Plants: Two General Electric J79-GE-10 turbojets each rated at 11,870 lb.s.t. and 17,860 lb.s.t. with afterburning.

Performance: Max. speed, 1,385 m.p.h. at 40,000 ft. (Mach 2·1); max. stabilised speed (without external stores), 1,254 m.p.h. (Mach 1·9); max. low-level cruise, 633 m.p.h. (Mach 0·83); long-range cruise, 560 m.p.h. at 40,000 ft. (Mach 0·85); operational ceil., 64,000 ft.; max. range, 2,995 mls.

Weights: Loaded, 61,730 lb.; max. overload, 80,000 lb.

Armament: The RA-5C normally fulfils the reconnaissance role but possesses secondary attack capability with ordnance on four external pylons.

Status: Production, originally terminated in 1963, reinstated in 1967 with order for additional 46 machines, first of these flying March 1969. Prototype RA-5C flown June 30, 1962.

Notes: The RA-5C carries an extremely sophisticated reconnaissance system, including vertical, oblique, and split-image cameras, and SLAR (Side-Looking Airborne Radar) in removable modules. Aircraft delivered from April 1969 have uprated J79-GE-10 engines and enlarged wing root leading edge fillets.

NORTH AMERICAN ROCKWELL
RA-5C VIGILANTE

Dimensions: Span, 53 ft. 0 in.; length, 75 ft. 10 in.; height, 19 ft. 4¾ in.; wing area, 769 sq. ft.

NORTHROP F-5

Country of Origin: U.S.A.

Type: Single-seat strike fighter and tandem two-seat advanced conversion trainer.

Power Plants: Two (F-5A/B) General Electric J85-GE-13 turbojets each rated at 2 720 lb.s.t. and 4,080 lb.s.t. with afterburning, or (CF-5A/D and NF-5A/B) two Orenda J85-Can-15 turbojets each rated at 2,920 lb.s.t. and 4,300 lb.s.t. with afterburning.

Performance: (Single-seater with J85-Can-15) Max. speed (at 11,630 lb.), 790 m.p.h. at sea level (Mach 1·04), 977 m.p.h. at 36,000 ft. (Mach 1·48); long-range cruise (max. external fuel), 560 m.p.h. at 36,000 ft.; ferry range (two 41·6 and three 125 Imp. gal. tanks), 1,580 mls.; tactical radius (333 Imp. gal. external fuel and 1,500 lb. ordnance for hi-lo-hi mission), 575 mls.; initial climb (at 11,630 lb.), 33,000 ft./min.

Weights: Empty equipped, 10,380 lb.; loaded (clean), 14,150 lb.; max. overload, 20,390 lb.

Armament: Two 20-mm. M-39 cannon with 280 r.p.g., and up to 6,200 lb. external ordnance.

Status: First prototype flown July 30, 1959, and first production May 19, 1964. Total of 728 (F-5A/B) ordered from parent company by beginning of 1970 of which 620 delivered. Eight-per-month production rate in 1970.

Notes: Joint manufacturing programme between Canada and Netherlands for production of 89 single-seat CF-5As and 26 two-seat CF-5Ds for former and 75 single-seat NF-5As and 30 two-seat NF-5Bs (illustrated above) for the latter. A camera nose is available (RF-5A) and illustrated opposite.

NORTHROP F-5

Dimensions: Span, 25 ft. 9 in.; length (over probe), 47 ft. 2⅛ in.; height, 13 ft. 2 in.; wing area, 173·82 sq. ft.

PILATUS PC-8D TWIN-PORTER

Country of Origin: Switzerland.
Type: Light STOL utility transport.
Power Plants: Two Lycoming IO-540-G1B5 six-cylinder horizontally-opposed engines each rated at 290 h.p.
Performance: (Estimated at 5,950 lb.) Max. speed, 162 m.p.h. at 8,000 ft.; max. cruise (70% power), 143 m.p.h. at 8,000 ft.; econ. cruise (65% power), 140 m.p.h.; max. range (with 1,590-lb. payload), 680 mls.; initial climb, 1,200 ft./min.
Weights: Empty, 3,420 lb.; max. take-off, 5,950 lb.
Accommodation: Pilot and nine passengers in pairs.
Status: First of two prototypes flown November 28, 1967. Redesign being undertaken in 1969.
Notes: Development of the Twin-Porter has been delayed pending a definitive choice of engines, and consideration is being given to the adaptation of the basic design to take turboprops. At the time of closing for press, various changes intended for the production model were being incorporated in a second prototype. Much of the airframe of the Twin-Porter is based on that of the single-engined PC-6 Porter, and similar short-take-off-and-landing characteristics are offered. Large double-doors are incorporated in each side of the fuselage to facilitate the loading of freight.

PILATUS PC-8D TWIN-PORTER

Dimensions: Span, 51 ft. 2½ in.; length, 34 ft. 7¼ in.; height, 12 ft. 0 in.; wing area, 348 sq. ft.

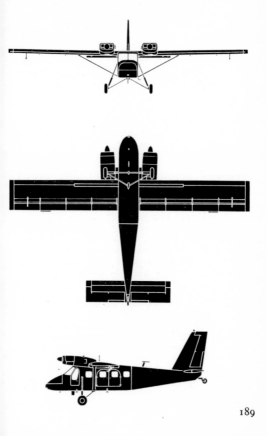

PIPER PA-35 POCONO

Country of Origin: U.S.A.

Type: Light executive transport and feederliner.

Power Plants: Two Lycoming TIO-720-A1A eight-cylinder horizontally-opposed engines each rated at 470 h.p.

Performance: (Estimated at 9,000 lb.) Max. speed, 242 m.p.h. at 10,000 ft.; max. cruise (75% power), 216 m.p.h. at 10,000 ft., 230 m.p.h. at 17,000 ft.; range with 45 min. reserves (at 75% power), 650 mls., (55% power), 810 mls.; initial climb, 1,630 ft./min.

Weights: Empty equipped (freighter), 4,650 lb., (18-seat feederliner), 4,900 lb.; max. take-off, 9,000 lb.

Accommodation: Basic arrangements for pilot and 13 or 17 passengers as feederliner, or crew of two and up to 11 passengers as executive transport.

Status: Prototype flown for first time on May 13, 1968, but production uncertain at time of closing for press.

Notes: The largest aircraft yet built by Piper, the Pocono is intended primarily for the third-level scheduled-service and light freighter market. The specification applies to the prototype (which is illustrated), but the production Pocono will have 520 h.p. engines and a gross weight of 9,750 lb. Modifications necessary to meet performance specifications have delayed commencement of production. These changes have included a 2-ft. increase in tailplane span, a lengthened fuselage and new wing root fillets.

PIPER PA-35 POCONO

Dimensions: Span, 51 ft. 0 in.; length, 39 ft. 3 in.; height, 15 ft. 9 in.; wing area, 315 sq. ft.

ROBIN HR 100

Country of Origin: France.

Type: Light cabin monoplane.

Power Plant: One Lycoming IO-540-D4A5 six-cylinder horizontally-opposed engine rated at 180 h.p.

Performance: Max. cruise (estimated at 3,086 lb.), 186 m.p.h. at 8,000 ft.; econ. cruise, 166 m.p.h.; range (at econ. cruise with normal reserves), 1,250 mls.

Weights: Empty equipped, 1,873 lb.; max. take-off, 3,086 lb.

Accommodation: Seating for pilot and three passengers in side-by-side pairs with individual seats at front and bench-type seat at rear.

Status: First of five prototypes flown April 3, 1969 with series production expected to commence in 1970.

Notes: The HR 100 is the first all-metal aircraft to be developed by Avions Pierre Robin (the former Centre Est Aéronautique) which has specialised in the design and manufacture of wood-and-fabric light aircraft since 1957. The prototypes of the HR 100 have been fitted initially with 180 h.p. Lycoming IO-360 four-cylinder engines to permit comparative trials with other Robin light aircraft of similar power, but all aircraft will eventually be re-engined with the IO-540-D4A5 intended for the series production model, and this higher-powered version is described by the specification above.

ROBIN HR 100

Dimensions: Span, 32 ft. 9¾ in.; length, 24 ft. 3¼ in.; height, 7 ft. 6½ in.; wing area, 176·53 sq. ft.

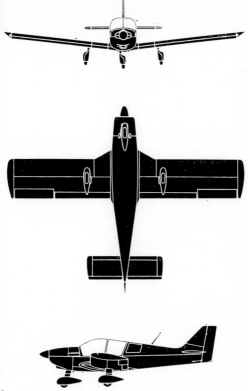

SAAB 105XT

Country of Origin: Sweden.

Type: Basic trainer and light strike and reconnaissance aircraft.

Power Plants: Two General Electric J85-GE-17B turbojets each rated at 2,850 lb.s.t.

Performance: Max. speed (at 8,818 lb.) 604 m.p.h. at sea level, 547 m.p.h. at 32,810 ft.; tactical radius with six 500-lb. bombs (lo-lo-lo mission), 200 mls., (hi-lo-hi), 514 mls., with four 500-lb. bombs and two 108 Imp. gal. drop tanks (lo-lo-lo), 325 mls., (hi-lo-hi), 845 mls., range (at 437 m.p.h. at 36,000 ft. with 20 min. reserves), 1,380 mls., (with two 108 Imp. gal. drop tanks), 1,715 mls.; initial climb (at 8,818 lb.), 12,795 ft./min., (at 10,802 lb.), 9,055 ft./min.; service ceil. (at 8,818 lb.), 44,950 ft.

Weights: Empty, 5,550 lb.; normal loaded (clean), 9,750 lb.; max. loaded, 14,328 lb.

Armament: Maximum of 4,410 lb. of ordnance on six underwing pylons. Typical loads include two 30-mm. cannon pods and two Sidewinder AAMs, four 500-lb. and two 1,000-lb. bombs, or 12 13·5-cm. rockets.

Status: In production. Prototype Saab 105XT flown April 29, 1967. First deliveries (against order for 40) to Austria scheduled Spring 1970.

Notes: The Saab 105XT is an export version of the basic Saab 105 which (with two 1,640 lb.s.t. Turbo-méca Aubisque turbofans) serves with the Swedish Air Force as the SK 60A trainer, SK 60B trainer with attack capability, and SK 60C trainer with attack and photo-reconnaissance capability.

194

SAAB 105XT

Dimensions: Span, 31 ft. 2 in.; length, 34 ft. 5⅓ in.; height, 8 ft. 10¼ in.; wing area, 175·515 sq. ft.

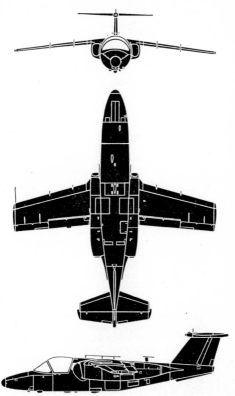

SAAB 35F DRAKEN

Country of Origin: Sweden.

Type: Single-seat interceptor fighter.

Power Plant: One SFA RM 6C (RB.146 Mk. 60 Avon) turbojet rated at 12,710 lb.s.t. and 17,260 lb.s.t. with afterburning.

Performance: Max. speed (clean aircraft at 22,900 lb.), 1,320 m.p.h. at 36,100 ft. (Mach 2·0), (with four Rb 27/28 AAMs at 23,100 lb.), 1,120 m.p.h. at 36,100 ft. (Mach 1·7); radius of action (hi-lo-hi mission profile on internal fuel), 350 mls., (with two 231 Imp. gal. external tanks), 600 mls.; max. climb (at 22,900 lb.), 39,500 ft./min.; time to 36,100 ft. (at 22,900 lb. from brakes off), 2·5 min., to 65,600 ft., 6·5 min.

Weights: Empty equipped, 16,800 lb.; loaded (clean aircraft), 22,900 lb.

Armament: One 30-mm. Aden M/55 cannon and (intercept) two semi-active radar-homing Rb 27 and two infra-red homing Rb 28 AAMs, or (secondary attack role) two 1,100-lb. or nine 220-lb. bombs, or 12 13·5-cm. Bofors rockets.

Status: (Saab 35F) Prototype airframe flown 1961 with first production delivery (to *Flygvapnet*) 1965. Production phasing out during 1970.

Notes: Saab 35F (J 35F) is definitive production version of the Draken. The export version, the Saab 35X (see 1969 edition), is being delivered to Denmark from spring 1970, 20 fighter-bomber, 20 reconnaissance-fighter and six two-seat trainer versions having been ordered by the Royal Danish Air Force. Approximately 550 Drakens of all types purchased for *Flygvapnet*.

SAAB 35F DRAKEN

Dimensions: Span, 30 ft. 10¾ in.; length (excluding probe), 46 ft. 10¼ in.; height, 12 ft. 8⅓ in.; wing area, 529·8 sq. ft.

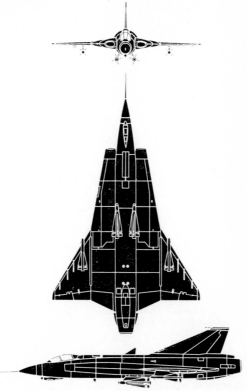

SAAB 37 VIGGEN

Country of Origin: Sweden.

Type: Single-seat (AJ 37) strike fighter and two-seat (Sk 37) advanced trainer.

Power Plant: One Svenska Flygmotor RM 8 (Pratt & Whitney JT8D-22) turbofan rated at approx. 16,000 lb.s.t. and 26,450 lb.s.t. with afterburning.

Performance: (Approximate at normal loaded weight) Max. speed, 835 m.p.h. at 330 ft. (Mach 1·1), 1,320 m.p.h. at 39,370 ft. (Mach 2·0); tactical radius (hi-lo-hi mission profile with typical ordnance load), 630 mls., (lo-lo-lo), 320 mls. time to 36,090 ft. at 33,060 lb., 2 min.; service ceil., 60,000 ft.

Weight: Normal loaded, 35,275 lb.

Armament: (Attack mission) Rb 04C or RB 05A attack missiles or pods containing six 13·5-cm. or 19 7·5-cm. rockets, or 30-mm. Aden cannon, or 1,000-lb. bombs on five external pylons. (Intercept mission) Rb 24 (Sidewinder), Rb 27 or Rb 28 (Falcon) AAMs.

Status: First of seven prototypes flown February 8, 1967, and six under test by end of 1970. Seventh prototype will be two-seat trainer. Production orders placed by beginning of 1970 for 175 aircraft. First delivery scheduled for July 1, 1971, with completion of initial order for 100 aircraft (83 AJ 37s and 17 Sk 37s) by beginning of 1974.

Notes: Versions of Viggen to be covered by follow-on contracts uncertain at time of closing for press but probably include the S 37 tactical reconnaissance aircraft, the future of the JA 37 interceptor with secondary attack capability being under review.

SAAB 37 VIGGEN

Dimensions: Span, 34 ft. 9½ in.; length (including nose probe), 53 ft. 5¾ in.; height, 18 ft. 4½ in.

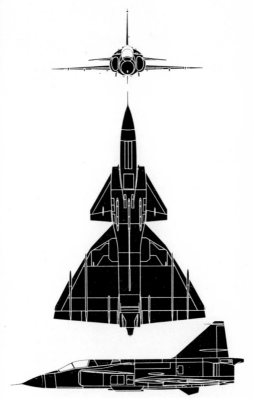

SHIN MEIWA PS-1

Country of Origin: Japan.
Type: Long-range maritime patrol flying boat.
Power Plants: Four General Electric T64-IHI-10 turboprops each rated at 2,850 e.s.h.p.
Performance: Max. speed, 340 m.p.h.; normal cruise, 196 m.p.h. at 4,920 ft.; initial climb, 2,264 ft./min.; max. ceil., 29,530 ft.; normal range, 1,347 mls.; max. range, 2,948 mls.
Weights: Operational empty, 51,852 lb.; max. take-off, 86,862 lb.
Armament: Max. of four 2,165-lb. torpedoes, six 5-in. HVAR missiles, or four 330-lb. depth bombs.
Status: First prototype flown November 6, 1967, and second on June 14, 1968. Two pre-production PS-1 flying boats to be delivered September 1971 and January 1972. These will be followed by 14 production aircraft.
Notes: The PS-1 (formerly PX-S) employs an airscrew slipstream deflection system and boundary-layer control, a 1,250 s.h.p. T58-IHI-8B turboshaft being carried for the latter. The high length-to-beam ratio claimed to provide exceptional seaworthiness, a grove-type spray suppressor evolved by the designer of the flying boat, Dr. Kikuhara, aiding operation in rough seas. The PS-1 has a normal crew of 12 members, and three six-aircraft squadrons are to be formed.

SHIN MEIWA PS-1

Dimensions: Span, 107 ft. 7⅓ in.; length, 109 ft. 10¾ in.; height, 31 ft. 9¾ in.; wing area, 1,453·13 sq. ft.

SHORT SC.5/10 BELFAST C. MK. 1

Country of Origin: United Kingdom.

Type: Military strategic transport.

Power Plants: Four Rolls-Royce Tyne R.Ty. 12 Mk. 101 turboprops each rated at 5,730 e.h.p.

Performance: Max. cruise (at 200,000 lb.) 338 m.p.h. at 28,000 ft.; long-range cruise, 315 m.p.h. at 24,000 ft.; initial climb, 1,060 ft./min.; service ceil., 30,000 ft.; range (30,000-lb. payload), 3,985 mls., (with max. payload—80,000 lb.), 1,000 mls. at 315 m.p.h. at 25,000 ft.

Weights: Basic operational, 127,000 lb.; max. take-off, 230,000 lb.

Accommodation: Flight crew of four plus air quarter-master. Typical military loads include three Alvis Saladin armoured cars, two Polaris-type missiles, three Wessex or four Whirlwind helicopters, or up to 80,000 lb. of freight for short-range tactical operations and 30,000 lb. in the strategic role.

Status: Production completed. First aircraft flown January 5, 1964, and 10th and last example late 1966.

Notes: Drag-reduction modifications on initial five aircraft delayed service introduction, but full-scale operation by No. 53 Squadron of the R.A.F.'s Air Support Command with part modified aircraft began in 1967, and delivery of fully modified aircraft began May 1968, modifications to all 10 aircraft being completed in 1969.

SHORT SC.5/10 BELFAST C. MK. 1

Dimensions: Span, 158 ft. 9½ in.; length, 136 ft. 5 in.; height, 47 ft. 0 in.; wing area, 2,466 sq. ft.

SHORT SKYVAN SERIES 3

Country of Origin: United Kingdom.
Type: Light utility transport.
Power Plants: Two Garrett AiResearch TPE 331-2-201A turboprops each rated at 757 e.s.h.p.
Performance: Max. cruise, 200 m.p.h. at 10,000 ft.; long-range cruise, 170 m.p.h. at 10,000 ft.; range with max. payload (4,600 lb), 190 mls.; range with max. fuel (and 2,894-lb. payload), 777 mls.; initial climb, 1,500 ft./min.; service ceil., (at 12,500 lb.), 21,000 ft.
Weights: Operational empty (freighter), 7,100 lb.; max. loaded, 12,500 lb.
Accommodation: Flight crew of two with maximum of 18 passengers, or 12 casualty stretchers and two medical attendants.
Status: First Skyvan Srs. 3 (conversion of third Srs. 2) flown December 15, 1967, and customer deliveries commenced summer 1968 with 40 scheduled for delivery by the beginning of 1970. Production rate of five per month is expected to be maintained throughout 1970.
Notes: The Srs. 3 has supplanted the Srs. 2 owing to the failure of the Turboméca Astazou XII engines of the latter to meet specified performance. Only eight Astazou-powered Srs. 2 aircraft were delivered, production of this model being abandoned. The military version of the Skyvan is cleared for overload operations up to 13,500 lb.

SHORT SKYVAN SERIES 3

Dimensions: Span, 63 ft. 11 in.; length, 40 ft. 1 in.; height, 15 ft. 1 in.; wing area, 373 sq. ft.

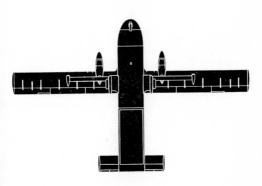

SIAI-MARCHETTI/FFA 202 BRAVO

Countries of Origin: Italy and Switzerland.
Type: Light cabin monoplane.
Power Plant: One Lycoming (AS/SA.202-10) O-235-C2A or (AS/SA.202-15) O-320-E2A four-cylinder horizontally-opposed engine rated at 115 and 150 h.p. respectively.
Performance: (AS/SA.202-10 with figures in parentheses relating to AS/SA.202-15) Max. speed (at 1,765 lb.), 141 (156) m.p.h.; cruise at 75% power and 1,874/1,974 lb.), 131 (141) m.p.h.; initial climb, 720 (1,050) ft./min.
Weights: Empty, 1,069 (1,102) lb.; max. take-off, 1,874 (1,984) lb.
Accommodation: Two persons side-by-side with dual controls, and (AS/SA.202-15) optional aft seat.
Status: Joint development by SIAI-Marchetti (Italy) and FFA (Switzerland) with former manufacturing wings, undercarriage and power plant installation, and latter producing fuselage, tail and controls, both concerns having assembly lines for complete aircraft. First Italian prototype flying May 8, 1969, having been preceded by first Swiss prototype on March 7, 1969. Production deliveries scheduled early 1970.
Notes: The Italo-Swiss Bravo has been designed primarily for use by schools and clubs, but is also potentially suitable for use as a military primary trainer.

SIAI-MARCHETTI/FFA 202 BRAVO

Dimensions: Span, 32 ft. 2 in.; length, 21 ft. 9¾ in.; height, 8 ft. 2¼ in.; wing area, 141·58 sq. ft.

SIAI-MARCHETTI S.208

Country of Origin: Italy.

Type: Light cabin monoplane.

Power Plant: One Lycoming O-540-E4A5 six-cylinder horizontally-opposed engine rated at 260 h.p.

Performance: Max. speed, 199 m.p.h. at sea level; cruise (75% power), 187 m.p.h. at 6,500 ft., (65% power), 176 m.p.h. at 8,200 ft.; service ceil., 21,000 ft.; max. range, 746 mls.

Weights: Empty, 1,720 lb.; max. take-off, 2,976 lb.

Accommodation: Basic accommodation for four persons in two pairs of side-by-side seats, with a collapsible seat installed in the baggage compartment for a fifth person.

Status: Prototype flown May 22, 1967. Initial series of 50 aircraft begun mid-1967 with first customer delivery early 1968. Production rate during 1969 (including lower-powered S.205) 16 per month.

Notes: The S.208 has been based on the lower-powered S.205 (see 1967 edition) and features individual rear seats in place of the bench of the earlier model, an optional fifth seat on which there are no weight restrictions, and a third window on each side of the fuselage. The S.208 is being marketed in the U.S.A. with a 250 h.p. Franklin 6AS-350A engine as the Waco TS250-5 Vega, and 24 S.208s have been delivered to the Italian Air Force for training and liaison tasks.

208

SIAI-MARCHETTI S.208

Dimensions: Span, 35 ft. 7¾ in.; length, 27 ft. 2¾ in.; height, 9 ft. 5¾ in.; wing area, 173·19 sq. ft.

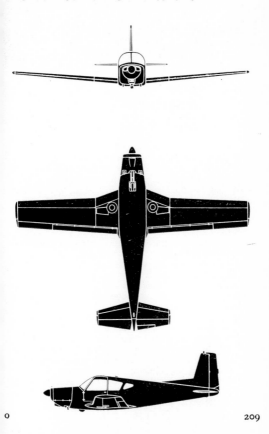

SIAI-MARCHETTI S.210

Country of Origin: Italy.
Type: Light cabin monoplane.
Power Plants: Two Lycoming TIO-360-A1B six-cylinder horizontally-opposed engines each rated at 200 h.p.
Performance: (Estimated) Max. speed, 222 m.p.h. at sea level; max. cruise, 211 m.p.h. at 8,000 ft.; econ. cruise, 195 m.p.h. at 8,000 ft.; range (with max. payload), 1,180 mls.; initial climb, 1,180 ft./min.; service ceil., 26,500 ft.
Weights: Empty equipped, 2,271 lb.; max. take-off, 4,078 lb.
Accommodation: Pilot and five passengers in three pairs of side-by-side seats.
Status: First prototype was scheduled to fly before the end of 1969. Second prototype, one static test specimen, three pre-series and 20 production aircraft in hand at beginning of 1970 with first deliveries scheduled during course of year.
Notes: The S.210 is a derivative of the single-engined S.205 series of light aircraft, and is intended to embody a number of structural components of the latter. A prototype was originally scheduled to fly before the end of 1967, but SIAI-Marchetti gave priority to launching and establishing the company's single-engined line of cabin monoplanes. The prototypes are powered by the 220 h.p. Lycoming TSIO-360 which is to be offered as an alternative to the TIO-360.

210

SIAI-MARCHETTI S.210

Dimensions: Span, 38 ft. 2 in.; length, 28 ft. 2½ in.;
height, 10 ft. 1¼ in.; wing area, 185·5 sq. ft.

SIAI-MARCHETTI SF.260

Country of Origin: Italy.
Type: Light cabin monoplane.
Power Plant: One Lycoming O-540-E4A5 six-cylinder
horizontally-opposed engine rated at 260 h.p.
Performance: Max. speed, 230 m.p.h. at sea level;
cruise (75% power), 222 m.p.h. at 6,500 ft., (65%
power), 215 m.p.h. at 10,000 ft.; initial climb rate,
1,800 ft./min.; service ceiling, 21,370 ft.; range,
1,050 mls.
Weights: Empty, 1,488 lb.; max. take-off (aerobatic),
2,200 lb.; (utility), 2,425 lb.
Accommodation: Three persons in two side-by-side
front seats and one person at rear.
Status: Production averaged six per month during 1969.
Notes: The prototype, known as the F.250 and powered
by a 250 h.p. Lycoming O-540-A1D, was flown July 15,
1964, and was built by Aviamilano. The second prototype, built by SIAI-Marchetti and powered by an uprated engine, was designated SF.260 and appeared in
1966. The SF.260 is fully aerobatic with two persons
and up to a gross weight of 2,200 lb. It has been
adopted as a trainer by the Sabena and Air France
schools, and 36 have been ordered for service with the
Belgian Air Force. The SF.260 is marketed in the
U.S.A. by Waco Aircraft as the SF260-3 Meteor.

SIAI-MARCHETTI SF.260

Dimensions: Span, 26 ft. 11¾ in.; length, 23 ft. 0 in.; height, 8 ft. 6 in.; wing area, 108·5 sq. ft.

SOCATA ST-10 DIPLOMATE

Country of Origin: France.

Type: Light cabin monoplane.

Power Plant: One Lycoming IO-360-C four-cylinder horizontally-opposed engine rated at 200 h.p.

Performance: Max. speed (at 2,689 lb.), 174 m.p.h. at sea level; max. cruise, 165 m.p.h.; max. range (with four persons), 746 mls. at econ. cruise; initial climb, 945 ft./min.; service ceil., 16,400 ft.

Weights: Empty equipped, 1,594 lb.; max. take-off, 2,689 lb.

Accommodation: Pilot and three passengers in pairs. Dual controls standard.

Status: First prototype flown November 7, 1967, and second early 1968. Production expected to commence 1970.

Notes: The ST-10, designed by SOCATA (Société de Construction d'Avions de Tourisme et d'Affaires), is a development of the GY-80 Horizon and possesses a similar wing and basically similar fuselage. The aircraft was initially known as the Super Horizon 200 and subsequently as the Provence, but in 1969 the name Diplomate was finally adopted. Production of the Diplomate has been delayed by the need to introduce a number of modifications, including a 1 ft. 4¾ in. fuselage extension, redesigned vertical tail surfaces, raised upper fuselage contours and tailplane, and undercarriage modifications.

214

SOCATA ST-10 DIPLOMATE

Dimensions: Span, 31 ft. 9¾ in.; length, 23 ft. 3½ in.; height, 9 ft. 5⅜ in.; wing area, 139·93 sq. ft.

SOCATA ST-60 RALLYE 7-300

Country of Origin: France.
Type: Light utility monoplane.
Power Plant: One Lycoming IO-540-K six-cylinder horizontally-opposed engine rated at 300 h.p.
Performance: Max. speed, 186 m.p.h.; cruise at 75% power, 174 m.p.h.; range, 870 mls. at 174 m.p.h.; initial climb rate, 984 ft./min.; service ceil., 16,400 ft.
Weights: Empty equipped, 1,854 lb.; max. take-off, 3,950 lb.
Accommodation: Pilot and six passengers. Passenger seats quickly removable to provide space for freight.
Status: Prototype flown for first time January 3, 1969. Production expected to be launched in 1970.
Notes: The Rallye 7-300 is the largest single-engined aircraft yet produced by SOCATA and, despite its name, bears little relationship to earlier Rallye aircraft apart from high lift devices. The Rallye 7-300 is claimed to possess exceptional short-field character-istics as a result of a combination of high engine power and large flaps, take-off and landing distances at maxi-mum weights being some 650 ft. and 490 ft. respect-ively. A second prototype will incorporate the changes to be introduced by the production model and resulting from discussions with potential customers. For freight-carrying operations the Rallye 7-300 is provided with a large cargo door.

216

SOCATA ST-60 RALLYE 7-300

Dimensions: Span, 36 ft. 1 in.; length, 29 ft. 5⅛ in.; wing area, 165·764 sq. ft.

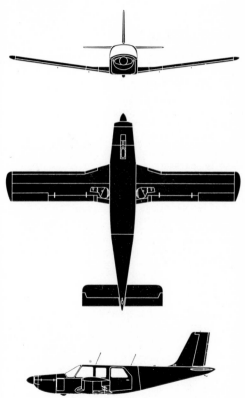

SUD-AVIATION CARAVELLE 12

Country of Origin: France.
Type: Medium-haul commercial transport.
Power Plants: Two Pratt & Whitney JT8D-9 turbofans each rated at 14,500 lb.s.t.
Performance: (Estimated) Max. cruise (at 110,230 lb.), 503 m.p.h. at 25,000 ft.; max. range (max. fuel and 18,850 lb. payload), 2,367 mls. at 30,000 ft., (with reserves for 230-mile diversion), 1,702 mls., (with 27,778-lb. payload and reserves for 230-mile diversion), 1,006 mls.
Weights: Empty, 65,036 lb.; operational empty, 71,430 lb.; max. take-off, 123,459 lb.
Accommodation: Normal flight crew of four and five-abreast seating for 118 or 128 tourist-class passengers, or mixed-class arrangement for 16 first-class and 88 tourist-class passengers.
Status: Caravelle scheduled to commence flight trials in 1970 with initial deliveries following in 1971. Approximately 260 Caravelles of all versions delivered by beginning of 1970, orders placed by the beginning of December 1969 calling for 269 aircraft (109 Type III, 53 Type VI-N, 56 Type VI-R, 19 Type 10-R, six Type 11-R, four Type 12, and 22 Super Caravelles).
Notes: The Caravelle 12 is essentially the Super Caravelle airframe with an additional 6 ft. 6¾ in. section inserted in the fuselage ahead of the wing and a 3 ft. 11½ in. section aft of the wing, the JT8D-7s being replaced by JT8D-9s.

SUD-AVIATION CARAVELLE 12

Dimensions: Span, 112 ft. 6½ in.; length, 118 ft. 10 in.; height, 28 ft. 7½ in.; wing area, 1,579 sq. ft.

SUD-NORD SN-600 CORVETTE

Country of Origin: France.
Type: Light business executive transport.
Power Plants: Two Pratt & Whitney JT15D-6 turbofans each rated at 2,200 lb.s.t.
Performance: (Estimated at 11,000 lb.) Max. cruise, 460 m.p.h. at 26,250 ft.; range (with eight passengers and 45 min. reserves), 1,070 mls. at max. cruise, 1,225 mls. at econ. cruise, (four passengers and 45 min. reserves), 1,510 mls. at max. cruise; initial climb (at 12,125 lb.), 3,350 ft./min.; service ceil., 40,000 ft.
Weights: Approx. empty equipped, 6,900 lb.; max. take-off, 12,499 lb.
Accommodation: Normal flight crew of two and standard arrangement for eight passengers in individual seats on each side of central aisle. Alternative arrangement for 10 or 13 passengers, and business executive layout for five–six passengers.
Status: Prototype scheduled to fly April 1970 with first customer deliveries planned for May 1972.
Notes: Developed as a result of collaboration between Sud-Aviation and Nord-Aviation, the Corvette is in a similar category to the Dassault Falcon 10 (see pages 72–73). The prototype is powered by JT15D-1 turbofans (the above specification relating to the initial production model), and the 2,300 lb.s.t. SNECMA-Turboméca Larzac turbofan is offered as an alternative. The Corvette is competing with the Falcon 10 for an *Armée de l'Air* order for 50–60 Larzac-powered aircraft.

SUD-NORD SN-600 CORVETTE

Dimensions: Span, 42 ft. 0 in.; length, 42 ft. 0 in.;
height, 14 ft. 4 in.; wing area, 236·8 sq. ft.

SUKHOI SU-7UTI (MOUJIK)

Country of Origin: U.S.S.R.

Type: Tandem two-seat ground attack fighter trainer.

Power Plant: One axial-flow turbojet rated at approx. 15,500 lb.s.t. and 22,050 lb.s.t with afterburning.

Performance: Max. speed (estimated at 25,000 lb. without external stores), 1,056 m.p.h. at 36,000 ft. (Mach 1·6), (estimated at 29,000 lb. with two rocket pods and two 132 Imp. gal. drop tanks), 790 m.p.h. (Mach 1·2); initial climb (at 25,000 lb.), 30,000 ft./min., (high drag configuration at 29,000 lb.), 23,500 ft./min.; range (with max. external fuel), 1,370 mls.

Weights: Estimated normal loaded, 25,000 lb.; max. loaded, 30,500 lb.

Armament: Two 30-mm. NR-30 cannon and four 550-lb. bombs on external pylons. Alternative loads include four pods each with 19 55-mm. rockets.

Status: The Su-7UTI is believed to have entered service during the early 'sixties, and production continues both for the Soviet Air Forces and for export.

Notes: The Su-7UTI is a tandem two-seat version of the Su-7M (Fitter) single-seat ground attack fighter (see 1969 edition) which has been in service with the Soviet Air Forces since the late 'fifties. Both single- and two-seat versions of the Su-7 have been extensively exported in recent years, and now serve with the air arms of Czechoslovakia, the German Democratic Republic, Poland, India, and the U.A.R.

SUKHOI SU-7UTI (MOUJIK)

Estimated Dimensions: Span, 32 ft. 3 in.; length, 55 ft.
0 in.; height, 15 ft. 9 in.

223

SUKHOI SU-11 (?) FLAGON-A

Country of Origin: U.S.S.R.
Type: Single-seat interceptor fighter.
Power Plants: Two turbojets each rated at approximately 15,500 lb.s.t. and 22,050 lb.s.t. with afterburning,
Performance: (Estimated) Max. speed, 1,650 m.p.h. at 40,000 ft. (Mach 2·5), 910 m.p.h. at sea level (Mach 1·2).
Weights: Approx. loaded, 50,000–55,000 lb.
Armament: Two air-to-air missiles on underwing pylons, possibly of Anab type.
Status: In production. Believed first entered operational service with Soviet Air Force in 1968.
Notes: Presumably intended as a successor to the Su-9 and possibly designated Su-11, this twin-jet all-weather interceptor may be considered as, in effect, an enlarged and considerably refined development of the Su-9, much of the design of the earlier aircraft, including the cockpit enclosure, undercarriage, delta wing, airbrake location, and vertical tail being retained. A short-take-off-and-landing version of the basic design (illustrated in the 1968 edition and dubbed Flagon-B) features two direct lift engines installed in the fuselage ahead of the propulsion units, two aft-hinged doors for these being provided in the upper fuselage decking, the exhaust outlets being covered by folding doors. In addition to the lift engine installation, the STOL version features extended outboard wing panels which, of reduced leading-edge sweep, result in a double-delta configuration.

224

SUKHOI SU-11 (?) FLAGON-A

Estimated Dimensions: Span, 33 ft. 6 in., length, 71 ft.
0 in.; height, 16 ft. 0 in.

SWEARINGEN MERLIN IIB

Country of Origin: U.S.A.

Type: Light executive transport.

Power Plants: Two Garrett-AiResearch TPE331-1-151G turboprops each rated at 665 s.h.p.

Performance: Cruise (at 10,000 lb.) 295 m.p.h. at 15,000 ft.; max. range, 1,785 mls. at 272 m.p.h. at 27,500 ft. with 45 min. reserves; initial climb, 2,570 ft./min.; service ceil., 29,900 ft.

Weights: Empty equipped, 6,450 lb.; max. take-off, 10,000 lb.

Accommodation: Crew of two on flight deck with dual controls, and standard accommodation for six passengers in main cabin.

Status: Prototype Merlin flown April 13, 1965, second prototype with lengthened fuselage (30 in.) flying a year later, and deliveries of initial model (Merlin IIA) began August 26, 1966. Thirty-six Merlin IIAs manufactured when type supplanted by Merlin IIB of which deliveries commenced September 1968 with more than 70 having been delivered by the beginning of 1970 when production was six per month.

Notes: Merlin IIB differs from IIA (550 s.h.p. PT6A-20 turboprops) in power plants and pressurisation system, and mates modified Beechcraft Queen Air wings and Twin Bonanza undercarriage with a completely new pressurised fuselage. Merlin IIA may be retro-fitted with 615 s.h.p. PT6A-27 engines.

SWEARINGEN MERLIN IIB

Dimensions: Span, 45 ft. 11 in.; length, 40 ft. 1¼ in.; height, 14 ft. 1 in.; wing area, 279·7 sq. ft.

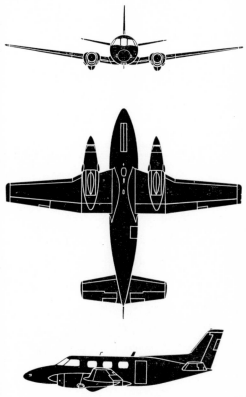

SWEARINGEN FS-226 METRO

Country of Origin: U.S.A.
Type: Short-haul commercial feederliner.
Power Plants: Two Garrett AiResearch TPE331-303 turboprops each rated at 904 e.s.h.p.
Performance: (Estimated at 12,500 lb.) Max. cruise, 300 m.p.h. at 20,000 ft.; range (3,900-lb. payload and 30 min. reserves with normal allowances), 300 mls. at max. cruise at 10,000 ft., (2,000-lb. payload), 950 mls. at 5,000 ft., 1,100 mls. at 10,000 ft., 1,500 mls. at 25,000 ft.
Weights: Empty equipped, 7,600 lb.; max. take-off, 12,500 lb.
Accommodation: Normal flight crew of two with 20 passengers in two-abreast seating. Movable bulkhead permitting variation of ratio of passengers to freight for mixed-traffic role.
Status: First definitive prototype flown August 26, 1969 with production deliveries scheduled to commence mid-1970. Fifty-nine firm orders plus six options placed by December 1969.
Notes: Developed in co-operation with Fairchild Hiller which is responsible for marketing, the Metro has been designed primarily for third-level or commuter type operations.

228

SWEARINGEN FS-226 METRO

Dimensions: Span, 46 ft. 3 in.; length, 59 ft. 4 in.; height, 16 ft. 7 in.; wing area, 277·5 sq. ft.

TRANSALL C.160

Country of Origin: France and Germany.
Type: Medium-range tactical transport.
Power Plants: Two Rolls-Royce Tyne R.Ty.20 Mk. 22 turboprops each rated at 5,665 s.h.p. (6,100 e.s.h.p.).
Performance: Max. cruise (at 90,390 lb.), 332 m.p.h. at 14,800 ft.; econ. cruise, 308 m.p.h. at 26,250 ft.; service ceil., 27,900 ft.; range (with max. payload—35,280 lb., and 10% reserves plus 30 min.), 1,070 mls., with max. fuel and 17,640-lb. payload), 3,010 mls.
Weights: Operational empty, 61,843 lb.; normal loaded, 97,440 lb.; max. take-off, 108,250 lb.
Accommodation: Crew of four and 81 troops or 62 casualty stretchers and four medical attendants. Other possible loads include armoured vehicles, tanks and tractors not exceeding 35,270 lb. weight.
Status: In production. First of three prototypes flown February 25, 1963, and first of six pre-production aircraft on May 21, 1965. Current orders call for 169 production aircraft (50 C.160Fs for France, 110 C.160Ds for Federal Germany, and nine C.160Zs for South Africa) of which first completed May 17, 1967. Production rate is three per month with VFW and HFB in Germany assembling 54 and 53 respectively, and Nord-Aviation in France assembling 62, current orders scheduled to be completed in 1972.
Notes: Joint Franco-German programme. Order for nine for South Africa negotiated 1966 scheduled to be completed April 1970, first deliveries to the South African Air Force being effected in August 1969.

TRANSALL C.160

Dimensions: Span, 131 ft. 2½ in.; length, 105 ft. 3½ in.;
height, 38 ft. 4¾ in.; wing area, 1,722·7 sq. ft.

TUPOLEV TU-22 (BLINDER-B)

Country of Origin: U.S.S.R.

Type: Long-range medium bomber and strike-reconnaissance aircraft.

Power Plants: Two turbojets rated at approximately 20,000 lb.s.t. and 27,000 lb.s.t. with afterburning.

Performance: (Estimated) Max. speed, 990 m.p.h. at 40,000 ft (Mach 1·5); max. cruise 630 m.p.h. at 40,000 ft.; unrefuelled tactical radius, 1,400 mls.; max. range, 4,000 mls.; service ceil., 60,000 ft.

Weights: Approx. loaded, 185,000 lb.

Armament: Free-falling weapons housed internally, or single semi-recessed Kitchen stand-off missile. Defensive: Single 23-mm. cannon in remotely controlled tail barbette.

Status: Believed to have attained operational status with the Soviet Air Force in 1965, and with shore-based elements of the Soviet naval air arm in 1967.

Notes: Successor to the subsonic Tu-16 (Badger) the Tu-22 was originally evolved by the Tupolev design bureau in the mid-'fifties as the *Samolet "Yu"* with the design bureau designation Tu-105. The most recent examples of the Tu-22 seen embody a number of modifications, these including an extended flight refuelling probe and enlarged engine air intakes, nacelles and exhaust orifices. Camera windows are provided in the nose and aft. A training version (Blinder-C) with a raised second cockpit for the instructor is in service, and is illustrated above and on opposite page.

232

TUPOLEV TU-22 (BLINDER-C)

Estimated Dimensions: Span, 91 ft. 0 in.; length
133 ft. 0 in.; height, 17 ft. 0 in.; wing area, 2,030 sq. ft.

233

TUPOLEV TU-28P (FIDDLER)

Country of Origin: U.S.S.R.

Type: Two-seat all-weather long-range interceptor and reconnaissance-strike aircraft.

Power Plants: Two turbojets each possessing an afterburning thrust of 24,000-25,000 lb.

Performance: (Estimated at a loaded weight of 78,000 lb.) Max. speed (without external ordnance), 1,060 m.p.h. at 39,370 ft., (with four Ash AAMs on external pylons), 925 m.p.h. at 39,370 ft.; tactical radius (high-altitude patrol mission), 900–1,100 mls., (hi-lo-hi strike mission), 650–700 mls.; service ceil., 60,000 ft.

Weights: Estimated normal loaded, 78,000 lb.; max. overload, 96,000 lb.

Armament: (Intercept) Four infra-red or radar-homing Ash AAMs on external pylons.

Status: First flown in prototype form in 1957 with first production deliveries to the Soviet Air Forces in early 'sixties. Believed currently in production.

Notes: The Tu-28 was originally evolved by the Tupolev design bureau to meet a long-range reconnaissance-strike aircraft requirement, and utilised a similar power plant arrangement to that of the experimental Tu-98 (Backfin) bomber of 1955. Biased towards economical high-altitude operation, the aircraft has since been developed primarily for the long-range intercept role as the Tu-28P, and one version carries its own early warning radar in ventral pack.

TUPOLEV TU-28P (FIDDLER)

Estimated Dimensions: Span, 65 ft. 0 in.; length, 90 ft. 0 in.

TUPOLEV TU-134A (CRUSTY)

Country of Origin: U.S.S.R.

Type: Short- and medium-haul commercial transport.

Power Plants: Two Soloviev D-30R turbofans each rated at 14,990 lb.s.t.

Performance: Max. cruise (at 94,800 lb.), 528 m.p.h. at 32,810 ft.; range cruise (at 103,617 lb.), 466 m.p.h. at 32,810 ft.; range (with 18,078-lb. payload at long-range cruise), 1,242 mls., (with 8,818-lb. payload), 2,175 mls.

Weights: Empty equipped, 63,934 lb.; max. take-off, 103,617 lb.

Accommodation: Basic flight crew of three and maximum of 84 passengers in four-abreast all-tourist class configuration.

Status: Prototype Tu-134 flown second half of 1962 with first production deliveries (to Aeroflot) in 1966. Stretched Tu-134A flown 1968 with first production deliveries commencing 1969.

Notes: The Tu-134A differs in several respects from the original Tu-134 (see 1969 edition) serving with Aeroflot, LOT, Balkan, Bulgarian, CSA, Interflug, Avio Genex, and Malev. The fuselage length has been increased by 9 ft. 8½ in., thrust reversers have been added to the engines, and the tail drag chute housing has been eliminated, its space being occupied by an auxiliary power unit. Some 50 Tu-134s were in service by the beginning of 1970.

TUPOLEV TU-134A (CRUSTY)

Dimensions: Span, 95 ft. 2 in.; length, 121 ft. 8¾ in.;
height, 29 ft. 7 in.; wing area, 1,370·3 sq. ft.

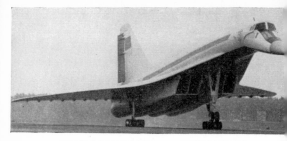

TUPOLEV TU-144 (CHARGER)

Country of Origin: U.S.S.R.

Type: Long-haul supersonic commercial transport.

Power Plants: Four Kuznetsov NK-144 turbofans each rated at 28,660 lb.s.t. and 38,580 lb.s.t. with afterburning.

Performance: (Estimated) Max. cruise, 1,550 m.p.h. at 49,200–65,600 ft. (Mach 2·35); service ceil., 65,600 ft.; max. ceil., 68,900 ft.; max. range, 4,040 mls.

Weights: Normal loaded, 286,660 lb.; max. take-off, 330,000 lb.

Accommodation: Basic flight crew of three and standard layout for 100 passengers in two cabins (forward cabin accommodating 18 passengers in three-abreast seating and aft cabin accommodating 82 in five- and four-abreast seating). Alternative layouts for 108 and 121 passengers.

Status: Two flying prototypes and one static test specimen to be followed by four pre-production examples and initial batch of 14 production aircraft. First prototype flown December 31, 1968, and service introduction by Aeroflot scheduled for late 1972.

Notes: The world's first supersonic transport to fly, and the first to exceed Mach 1·0 (June 5, 1969), the Tu-144 is claimed to be capable of operating at costs matching those of contemporary long-haul subsonic transports. Like the Concorde (see pages 24–25), it employs an ogival delta wing, and a droopable nose for take-off and landing.

TUPOLEV TU-144 (CHARGER)

Dimensions: Span, 75 ft. 5½ in.; length, 196 ft. 10¼ in.;
height, 37 ft. 0 in.; wing area, 3,982·65 sq. ft.

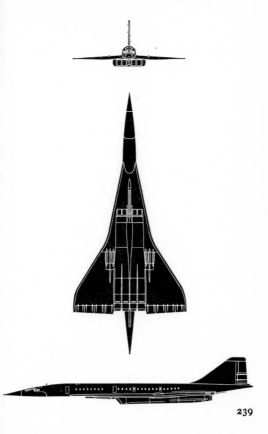

TUPOLEV TU-154 (CARELESS)

Country of Origin: U.S.S.R.
Type: Medium-range commercial transport.
Power Plants: Three Kuznetsov NK-8-2 turbofans each rated at 20,940 lb.s.t.
Performance: Max. cruise 564 m.p.h. at 39,370 ft.; econ. cruise, 484 m.p.h.; range (with 35,840-lb. payload and 1 hr. reserves), 2,100 mls. at 550 m.p.h. at 36,000 ft., (with 23,520-lb. payload), 3,730 mls.
Weights: Empty, 88,626 lb.; normal take-off (initial), 176,370 lb., (definitive), 189,598 lb.; max. take-off, 198,450 lb.
Accommodation: Three crew members and 152 tourist-class passengers. Alternative versions provide accommodation for 164 economy-class passengers or 24 tourist- and 104 economy-class passengers. A proposed freighter variant will carry up to 56,000 lb. of cargo.
Status: First prototype flown October 4, 1968. Five additional aircraft were scheduled to join the development programme by the end of 1969 with first deliveries to Aeroflot scheduled for 1970.
Notes: Intended as a successor to the Tu-104 in Aeroflot service, the Tu-154 is expected to commence route flying late 1970. A stretched version, the Tu-154M, accommodating 220–240 passengers and having uprated NK-8 turbofans is currently planned for service from 1972–73.

TUPOLEV TU-154 (CARELESS)

Dimensions: Span, 123 ft. 2⅓ in.; length, 157 ft. 1¾ in.; height, 37 ft. 4¾ in.; wing area, 2,168·92 sq. ft.

VFW-FOKKER VFW 614

Country of Origin: Federal Germany.
Type: Short-haul commercial transport.
Power Plants: Two Rolls-Royce/SNECMA M45H turbofans each rated at 7,700 lb.s.t.
Performance: (Estimated at 38,030 lb.) Max. cruise, 457 m.p.h. at 21,000 ft.; max. fuel range at 390 m.p.h. (with normal reserves), 1,785 mls.; range (40 passengers and normal reserves), 714 mls.; initial climb, 3,600 ft./min.; service ceil., 25,000 ft.
Weights: Operational empty, 24,250 lb.; max. take-off, 38,030 lb.
Accommodation: Normal flight crew of two and alternative arrangements for 36, 40 or 44 passengers in four-abreast seating.
Status: First of three prototypes scheduled to be rolled out late 1970 and commence flight test programme February 1971, followed by first customer deliveries late 1972.
Notes: The VFW 614 is being manufactured as a collaborative venture under the leadership of VFW-Fokker, participants including the Dutch VFW-Fokker branch, and SABCA and Fairey in Belgium. Options on the VFW 614 had been taken by Sterling Airways, Bavaria Fluggesellschaft, Transportees Aeros Buenos Aires, General Air, and Filipinas Orient Airways by mid-1969. An unconventional feature of this short-haul transport is the over-wing engine pod installation. Emphasis is placed on flexibility of operation in a wide variety of different environments and with a minimum of maintenance.

VFW-FOKKER VFW 614

Dimensions: Span, 70 ft. 6½ in.; length, 67 ft. 5¾ in.; height, 25 ft. 8 in.; wing area, 688·89 sq. ft.

VFW-FOKKER VAK 191B

Country of Origin: Federal Germany.
Type: Single-seat V/STOL strike fighter.
Power Plants: One Rolls-Royce/MTU Munchen RB.193–12 vectored thrust turbofan rated at 10,150 lb.s.t., and (lift) two Rolls-Royce RB.162-81 turbojets each rated at 5,568 lb.s.t.
Performance: (Estimated) Max. speed, 730 m.p.h. (Mach 0·96) at 1,000 ft., 605 m.p.h. (Mach 0·92) at 40,000 ft.; tactical radius (lo-lo-lo mission with full internal weapons load), 230 mls. at 610 m.p.h. (Mach 0·8).
Weights: Empty, 10,100 lb.; max. loaded (for vertical take-off), 16,530 lb., (short-take-off), 19,840 lb.
Armament: Internal bay for interchangeable packs containing two 30-mm. cannon and ammunition, retractible rocket launchers, bombs, reconnaissance equipment, or auxiliary fuel. Up to six weapons attachment points may be provided on the fuselage and a further four beneath the wings.
Status: Three prototypes under construction with first scheduled to fly February 1970.
Notes: As a result of changes in German strategy, the VAK 191B programme is now considered purely experimental and will proceed no further than prototype evaluation. All three prototypes are expected to be available by 1971 for use as system test-beds in connection with the Panavia (MRCA-75) Panther multi-purpose fighter.

VFW-FOKKER VAK 191B

Dimensions: Span, 20 ft. 2½ in.; length (excluding probe), 48 ft. 3½ in.; height, 14 ft. 0¾ in.; wing area, 134·5 sq. ft.

YAKOVLEV YAK-28P (FIREBAR)

Country of Origin: U.S.S.R.

Type: Two-seat all-weather interceptor fighter.

Power Plants: Two Tamansky R.37F turbojets each rated at approx. 13,200 lb.s.t. with full afterburning.

Performance: (Estimated with two Anab AAMs) Max. speed, 720 m.p.h. at sea level (Mach 0·95), 730 m.p.h. at 40,000 ft. (Mach 1·1); tactical radius (intercept mission with two AAMs), 600 mls.; max. range (with underwing pinion tanks), 1,750 mls.

Weights: Approx. normal loaded, 32,000 lb.

Armament: Two Anab infra-red or semi-active radar homing AAMs.

Status: Prototypes (Yak-28R) flown in 1960 with production deliveries (both Yak-28R and Yak-28P) commencing 1962–63. Production believed completed 1967–68.

Notes: Widely used by the Soviet Air Forces, the Yak-28P is representative of the third generation of Yak-25 (Flashlight-A) derivatives, the second generation being represented by the Yak-27P (Flashlight-C) and Yak-26 (Flashlight-D), other variants being the Yak-28 (Brewer) reconnaissance and strike aircraft, the Yak-28L and the Yak-28Y.

246

YAKOVLEV YAK-28P (FIREBAR)

Estimated Dimensions: Span, 38 ft. 6 in.; length, 59 ft. o in.; height, 13 ft. o in.; wing area, 400 sq. ft.

YAKOVLEV YAK-40 (CODLING)

Country of Origin: U.S.S.R.

Type: Short-haul commercial transport.

Power Plants: Three Ivchenko AI-25 turbofans each rated at 3,307 lb.s.t.

Performance: Max. speed (at 30,208 lb.), 466 m.p.h. at 17,000 ft.; econ. cruise, 342 m.p.h. at 19,685 ft.; range (with 5,080-lb. payload and 45 min. reserves), 622 mls., (max. fuel and 3,140-lb. payload), 920 mls.; initial climb, 2,000 ft./min.

Weights: Empty equipped, 20,600 lb.; normal take-off, 28,996 lb.; max. take-off, 30,208 lb.

Accommodation: Basic flight crew of two and alternative cabin configurations for 16, 20, or 24 passengers in three-abreast seating. High-density arrangement for 31 passengers without baggage. Also available as 8/10-passenger business executive transport.

Status: First of five prototypes flown October 21, 1966, and first production deliveries (to Aeroflot) mid-1968.

Notes: Development of a stretched version, the Yak-40A, initiated 1969 for 1972 service introduction with an additional 3 ft. 3½ in. section fore and aft of the wing and AI-25 turbofans uprated to 3,850 lb.s.t. The Yak-40A will provide accommodation for 33 passengers with normal baggage allowance for 40 passengers without baggage.

248

YAKOVLEV YAK-40 (CODLING)

Dimensions: Span, 82 ft. 0¼ in.; length, 66 ft. 3 in.;
height, 20 ft. 11 in.; wing area, 753·473 sq. ft.

YAKOVLEV FREEHAND

Country of Origin: U.S.S.R.

Type: Single-seat vertical-take-off-and-landing development aircraft.

Power Plants: Two 7,000–9,000 lb.s.t. vectored-thrust turbofans.

Performance: (Estimated) Max. speed, 645 m.p.h. at sea level (Mach 0·85); max. cruise, 500 m.p.h. at 5,000 ft. (Mach 0·8); tactical radius (VTOL), 100–150 mls. at sea level (STOL), 150–200 mls.

Weights: Approximate max. (STOL), 18,000 lb.

Status: Believed experimental only. Possibly serving as basis for operational lightweight V/STOL strike and reconnaissance aircraft.

Notes: Publicly revealed at Domodedovo in July 1967 when two examples were seen, this vertical-take-off-and-landing aircraft has been attributed to the design bureau of Alexander Yakovlev, although its origin was not known with certainty at the time of closing for press. Of cropped-delta configuration with bicycle-type main undercarriage members and forward-retracting outrigger stabilising wheels, the aircraft has side-by-side turbofans exhausting through two swivelling nozzles at the centre of gravity. Stabilisation in hover is provided by four puffer pipes, one at each wingtip, one in the boom protruding from the nose, and one beneath the tail. It is to be assumed that in the case of failure of one turbofan the gas stream from the remaining powerplant can be ducted to both nozzles. One of the examples of this aircraft seen at Domodedovo was equipped to carry underwing ordnance.

YAKOVLEV FREEHAND

Estimated Dimensions: Span, 27 ft. 0 in.; length (including nose boom), 57 ft. 0 in. (excluding nose boom), 47 ft. 0 in.; height, 15 ft. 0 in.

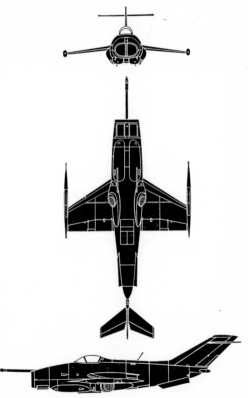

ZLIN Z-43

Country of Origin: Czechoslovakia.

Type: Light cabin monoplane.

Power Plant: One Avia M337 six-cylinder inverted inline engine rated at 210 h.p.

Performance: (At 2,557 lb.) Max. speed, 155 m.p.h. at sea level; max. cruise, 130 m.p.h.; range, 466 mls. at econ. cruise at 4,925 ft., (with two 11 Imp. gal. wingtip tanks), 1,200 mls.; initial climb, 985 ft./min.; service ceil., 18,050 ft.

Weights: Empty equipped, 1,543 lb.; normal take-off, 2,755 lb.; max. take-off, 2,976 lb.

Accommodation: Four persons in side-by-side pairs with individual seats forward and bench-type seat at rear.

Status: First of two prototypes flown November 1968 with first customer deliveries scheduled for mid-1971.

Notes: The Z-43 is the second in a new series of all-metal light aircraft produced by the Moravan works at Otrokovice, the first being the two-seat Z-42 (see 1969 edition) with which the Z-43 shares some 80% commonality of structural components. Like the Z-42, the Z-43 is stressed for aerobatic flight, but not to the same high *g* limits as the two-seater. Apart from the insertion of an extra steel-tube and glass-fibre section amidships, the fuselage of the Z-43 is similar to that of the Z-42.

252

ZLIN Z-43

Dimensions: Span, 32 ft. 0¼ in.; length, 25 ft. 5 in.;
height, 8 ft. 8¼ in.; wing area, 156·1 sq. ft.

AGUSTA A 106

Country of Origin: Italy.
Type: Single-seat light shipboard attack helicopter.
Power Plant: One Turboméca-Agusta TAA 230 turbo-shaft rated at 330 s.h.p.
Performance: (At 2,954 lb.) Max. speed, 110 m.p.h.; max. cruise, 105 m.p.h.; max. inclined climb, 1,230 ft./min.; hovering ceil. (in ground effect), 8,350 ft., (out of ground effect), 3,700 ft.; max. range (internal fuel), 155 mls.
Weights: Empty equipped, 1,520 lb.; normal loaded, 2,954 lb.; max. loaded, 3,086 lb.
Dimensions: Rotor diameter, 31 ft. 2 in.; fuselage length, 26 ft. 3 in.; overall height, 8 ft. 2½ in.
Notes: The A 106, the first of two prototypes of which flew in November 1965 and which was expected to enter production in 1970, is intended for use by Italy's *Marinavia*, and will be employed in the anti-submarine and anti-torpedo boat roles from *Doria* and *Alpino* class vessels. Offensive armament will consist of two Mk. 44 torpedoes, Julie acoustic echo ranging equipment will be fitted, and provision is made for external auxiliary fuel tanks. An enlarged version, the A 106B capable of carrying four persons over 230 miles at 115 m.p.h., is under development.
254

BELL 205A (UH-1H IROQUOIS)

Country of Origin: U.S.A.

Type: Utility and transport helicopter.

Power Plant: One Lycoming T53-L-13 turboshaft rated at 1,400 s.h.p.

Performance: Max. speed (at 9,025 lb.), 138 m.p.h.; max. cruise, 136 m.p.h.; normal range (at 9,025 lb.), 327 mls.; max. inclined climb, 1,760 ft./min.; hovering ceil. (in ground effect), 20,000 ft., (out of ground effect), 15,600 ft.

Weights: Empty, 4,850 lb.; normal loaded, 9,500 lb.

Dimensions: Rotor diameter, 48 ft. 0 in.; fuselage length, 42 ft. 0 in.; overall height, 14 ft. 4½ in.

Notes: The UH-1H Iroquois is the principal current production version of the Model 205A utility helicopter, and is essentially similar to the UH-1D apart from having a T53-L-13 turboshaft in place of the T53-L-11 derated to 1,100 s.h.p. The UH-1H can accommodate 12 troops, six casualty litters and a medical attendant, or 4,000 lb. of freight, and 2,074 examples of this variant of the Iroquois had been ordered by the end of 1968. The UH-1D Iroquois is manufactured under licence in Italy and Federal Germany, and is distinguished from the earlier UH-1B primarily in providing greater cabin space. The licence manufacture of the UH-1H in Formosa (Taiwan) will commence in 1970.

255

BELL 206A JETRANGER

Country of Origin: U.S.A

Type: Five-seat utility helicopter.

Power Plant: One Allison 250-C18 turboshaft rated at 317 s.h.p.

Performance: Max. speed, 150 m.p.h.; cruise (at 2,900 lb.), 134 m.p.h.; max. inclined climb, 1,600 ft./min.; hovering ceil. (in ground effect), 8,800 ft., (out of ground effect), 4,200 ft.; range 359 mls. at 137 m.p.h.

Weights: Empty, 1,295 lb.; loaded, 2,900 lb.

Dimensions: Rotor diameter, 33 ft. 4 in.; fuselage length, 28 ft. 2 in.; overall height, 9 ft. 6 in.

Notes: The JetRanger, the prototype of which was flown for the first time on January 10, 1966, is a derivative of Bell's unsuccessful entry in the original U.S. Army LOH (Light Observation Helicopter) contest. Two additional prototypes have been used in the development programme, and the first production JetRanger deliveries were effected in January 1967. Lighter and faster than its LOH predecessor, the OH-4A, the JetRanger has a refined structure, and in a re-opened LOH contest in 1968, a contract was awarded by the U.S. Army for JetRangers under the designation OH-58A Kiowa (illustrated). Forty have been delivered to U.S. Navy as TH-57A SeaRangers.

BELL 209 (AH-1G HUEYCOBRA)

Country of Origin: U.S.A.
Type: Two-seat attack helicopter.
Power Plant: One Lycoming T53-L-13 turboshaft rated at 1,250 s.h.p.
Performance: Max. speed (at 8,624 lb.), 186 m.p.h.; cruise, 166 m.p.h.; normal range (at 8,624 lb.), 425 mls.; max. inclined climb (at 8,624 lb.), 1,900 ft./min.; hovering ceil. (in ground effect), 18,600 ft., (out of ground effect), 11,900 ft.
Weights: Empty, 5,510 lb.; normal loaded, 8,624 lb.
Dimensions: Rotor diameter, 44 ft. 0 in.; fuselage length, 44 ft. 4¾ in.; overall height, 13 ft. 7¼ in.
Armament: One TAT-103 nose turret with one 7·62-mm. GAU-2B/A Minigun with 8,000 rounds, plus four XM-159 packs of 19 70-mm. rockets, four XM-157 packs of seven 70-mm. rockets, two XM-18 gun pods each with one 7·62-mm. Minigun, or six TOW wire-guided missiles.
Notes: The Model 209, or AH-1G, was first deployed in Vietnam by U.S. Army in 1967, and a total of 838 helicopters of this type had been ordered for the service by the end of 1969. The AH-1J SeaCobra is a U.S. Marine Corps version with PT6T-400 "Twin Pac" power plant, 49 having been ordered for 1970 delivery. The U.S.M.C. has received 38 AH-1Gs (illustrated).

BOEING-VERTOL CH-46D SEA KNIGHT

Country of Origin: U.S.A.

Type: Medium transport and assault helicopter.

Power Plants: Two General Electric T58-GE-10 turbo shafts each rated at 1,400 s.h.p.

Performance: Max. speed (at 20,800 lb.), 166 m.p.h. at sea level; long range cruise (at 23,000 lb.), 15 m.p.h.; tactical radius, 115 mls.; max. inclined climb (at 20,800 lb.), 1,900 ft./min.; hovering ceil. (at 20,800 lb. out of ground effect), 5,600 ft.

Weights: Empty, 13,067 lb.; max. loaded, 23,000 lb.

Dimensions: Rotor diameter (each), 51 ft. 0 in.; fuselage length, 44 ft. 10 in.; overall height, 16 ft. 11½ in.

Notes: The CH-46D and UH-46D are respectively U.S. Marine Corps logistic support and assault, and U.S. Navy medium utility and transport helicopters, these differing from the earlier CH-46A and UH-46A in having uprated turboshafts, cambered rotor blades with formation tip lights, provision for armour and armament. The CH-46D may accommodate up to 25 troops or 15 casualty litters and two medical attendants. More than 500 CH/UH-46s have been delivered, and licence manufacture of the basic Model 107 is undertaken in Japan by Kawasaki for both commercial operators and for the Japanese armed forces.

258

BOEING-VERTOL CH-47C CHINOOK

Country of Origin: U.S.A.

Type: Medium tactical transport helicopter.

Power Plants: Two Lycoming T55-L-11 turboshafts each rated at 3,750 s.h.p.

Performance: Max. speed, 184 m.p.h. at 5,000 ft.; max. radius of action (at 33,000 lb), 214 mls.; max. inclined climb, 2,740 ft./min.; hovering ceil. (out of ground effect), 13,850 ft.; service ceil. 19,500 ft.

Weights: Empty, 20,026 lb.; normal loaded, 33,000 lb.; maximum loaded, 44,800 lb.

Dimensions: Rotor diameter (each), 60 ft. 0 in.; fuselage length, 51 ft. 0 in.; overall height, 18 ft. 6½ in.

Notes: First flown on October 14, 1967, the CH-47C supplanted in production the CH-47B from which it differs solely in the model of the T55 turboshaft installed, the earlier variant of the Chinook having 2,850 s.h.p. T55-L-7C engines. The more powerful engines result in a 25% increase in payload capability and enable the CH-47C to transport loads weighing up to 23,400 lb. The U.S. Army took delivery of the first CH-47C in March 1968, and by the end of 1969 more than 550 Chinooks had been delivered, the first having entered service in 1963. An armed version of the earlier CH-47A has been tested in Vietnam, and 12 CH-47s are to be delivered to the Australian Army.

259

DORNIER DO 132

Country of Origin: Federal Germany.
Type: Light utility helicopter.
Power Plant: One Pratt & Whitney PT6A-20 hot gas
generator rated at 558 s.h.p.
Performance: (Estimated at 3,150 lb.) Max. speed,
186 m.p.h.; normal cruise, 133 m.p.h.; hovering ceil.
(out of ground effect), 3,280 ft.; normal range, 280 mls.
Weights: Empty, 1,490 lb.; normal loaded, 3,150 lb.;
max., 3,595 lb.
Dimensions: Rotor diameter, 35 ft. 0 in.; fuselage
length, 23 ft. 0 in.; overall height, 9 ft. 2½ in.
Notes: Scheduled to commence its flight test programme during the course of 1970, the Do 132 employs a hot cycle rotor system of semi-rigid two-blade
type. The hot gas generated by the turbine is fed
through apertures in the rotor head to blade ducts,
being ejected through blade-tip nozzles. The Do 132
has been proposed as a potential successor to the
Alouette II in service with the German armed forces,
and a contract for the construction and testing of three
prototypes has been awarded by the Federal Defence
Ministry. The Do 132 will compete in the 1972 light
observation helicopter replacement contest.

FAIRCHILD HILLER FH 1100

Country of Origin: U.S.A.

Type: Four-seat utility helicopter.

Power Plant: One Allison 250-C18 turboshaft rated at 275 s.h.p.

Performance: Max. speed, 127 m.p.h. at sea level; max. cruise, 127 m.p.h. at 5,000 ft.; max. inclined climb (at 2,530 lb.), 1,690 ft./min.; hovering ceil. (in ground effect), 15,950 ft., (out of ground effect), 11,100 ft.; service ceil., 16,400 ft.; max. range, 410 mls.

Weights: Empty, 1,395 lb.; max. loaded, 2,750 lb.

Dimensions: Rotor diameter, 35 ft. 5 in.; fuselage length, 29 ft. 9½ in.; overall height, 9 ft. 4¾ in.

Notes: The FH 1100 is a commercial derivative of the OH-5A which was the runner-up in the U.S. Army's first LOH (Light Observation Helicopter) contest, and the first production model was rolled out in April 1966. A somewhat more sophisticated helicopter than the Hughes winning entry in the initial LOH contest, the FH 1100 has hydraulically-boosted cyclic and collective pitch controls, and has been test flown in level flight at 160 m.p.h., although for maximum turbine efficiency cruise and red-lined speeds are identical at 127 m.p.h. Basically a four-seater, the FH 1100 is also available in five-seater form.

HUGHES MODEL 500 (OH-6A CAYUSE)

Country of Origin: U.S.A.

Type: Four-seat light observation and utility helicopter.

Power Plant: One Allison T63-A-5A turboshaft rated at 252 s.h.p.

Performance: Max. speed (at 2,400 lb.), 143 m.p.h. at sea level; econ. cruise, 134 m.p.h.; max. inclined climb, 1,560 ft./min.; hovering ceil. (out of ground effect), 7,600 ft.; service ceil., 15,550 ft.; range, 413 mls.

Weights: Empty, 1,156 lb.; normal loaded, 2,400 lb.; maximum overload, 2,700 lb.

Dimensions: Rotor diameter, 26 ft. 3 in.; fuselage length, 23 ft. 0 in.; overall height, 8 ft. 8½ in.

Notes: The Model 500 was, in its military form (to which the above specification applies), pronounced winner of the U.S. Army's first LOH (Light Observation Helicopter) contest in 1965, and deliveries commenced in September 1966, total orders for 1,415 having been placed for completion by December 1969. Licence manufacture of the OH-6A is being undertaken in Japan, after delivery of 17 helicopters to Kawasaki by the parent company late 1968, and in Italy by Nardi. The commercial Model 500 is a five-seater. The OH-6A is illustrated with two torpedoes.

KAMOV KA-25K (HORMONE)

Country of Origin: U.S.S.R.
Type: General-purpose and utility helicopter.
Power Plants: Two Glushenkov turboshafts each rated
at 900 e.h.p.
Performance: Max. speed, 137 m.p.h.; normal cruise,
121 m.p.h.; normal range (with 12 passengers), 248
mls.; range with auxiliary fuel, 404 mls.; range with
4,410-lb. slung load, 31 mls.
Weights: Normal loaded, 15,653 lb.; max. loaded,
16,094 lb.
Dimensions: Rotor diameter (each), 51 ft. 7½ in.;
fuselage length, 32 ft. 3 in.; overall height, 17 ft. 7⅜ in.
Notes: A multi-purpose helicopter evolved from the
Ka-20 experimental anti-submarine warfare helicopter,
the Ka-25K was under test in prototype form in 1967.
Capable of accommodating up to 12 passengers or a
maximum freight load of 4,410 lb., the latter being
slung beneath the fuselage, the Ka-25K featured an hy-
draulic winch, the winch operator being accommodated
in an aft-facing glazed gondola beneath the fuselage
nose. The turboshaft engines are mounted side-by-
side above the cabin. An assault transport and anti-
submarine warfare version is employed by the Soviet
Navy aboard the helicopter carriers *Moskva* and
Leningrad. This features a lengthened fuselage.

263

KAMOV KA-26 (HOODLUM)

Country of Origin: U.S.S.R.
Type: Light utility helicopter.
Power Plants: Two Vedeneev M-14V-26 air-cooled radial engines each rated at 325 h.p.
Performance: Max. speed, 106 m.p.h.; max. cruise, 84 m.p.h.; econ. cruise, 62 m.p.h.; hovering ceil. at 6,614 lb. (in ground effect), 4,068 ft., (out of ground effect), 2,625 ft.; service ceil., 9,843 ft.; range (with seven passengers), 250 mls. at 1,640 ft., with auxiliary tanks, 746 mls.
Weights: Operational empty, 4,300 lb.; loaded, 6,614 lb., (agricultural version), 6,966 lb.
Dimensions: Rotor diameter (each), 42 ft. 8 in.; fuselage lenght, 25 ft. 5½ in.; overall height, 13 ft. 3 in.
Notes: The Ka-26, which appeared in 1965, is a multipurpose helicopter which features a removable cabin for six passengers, two casualty stretchers, two sitting casualties and a medical attendant, or freight. The passenger cabin may be replaced by an open platform for bulky cargo loads, and an agricultural version can carry 1,984 lb. of dry chemicals or a tank for an equivalent quantity of liquid chemical. The plastic and fibreglass rotor blades are interchangeable. Production deliveries began in 1966, and the helicopter was exported to Hungary and Bulgaria in 1968–69.

MBB BÖ 105

Country of Origin: Federal Germany.
Type: Light utility helicopter.
Power Plants: Two MTU Munchen 6022-701-A3 turboshafts each rated at 375 s.h.p.
Performance: (Estimated) Max. speed, 155 m.p.h.; max. cruise, 143 m.p.h.; max. inclined climb, 2,060 ft./min.; hovering ceil. (in ground effect), 15,090 ft.; (out of ground effect), 11,480 ft.; service ceil., 18,700 ft.; normal range, 440 mls., (with auxiliary fuel), 858 mls. at 6,600 ft.
Weights: Empty, 2,360 lb.; loaded, 4,410 lb.
Dimensions: Rotor diameter, 32 ft. 2 in.; fuselage length, 28 ft. 0½ in.; overall height, 9 ft. 9⅜ in.
Notes: The first prototype of the Bö 105 powered by a pair of Allison 250-C18 turboshafts and equipped with a Westland Scout articulated blade rotor system was destroyed as a result of resonance during ground trials. The similarly-powered second prototype flew on February 16, 1967, and differed in having the Bölkow rigid rotor system with lightweight glass-fibre-reinforced plastic blades. The third prototype, flown December 20, 1967, is described above; two pre-production examples flew during 1969, and production deliveries (by SIAT) will begin 1970.

MIL MI-2 (HOPLITE)

Country of Origin: U.S.S.R. (Licence-built in Poland).
Type: Light utility helicopter.
Power Plants: Two Izotov GTD-350 turboshafts each rated at 400 s.h.p.
Performance: Max. speed, 137 m.p.h.; econ. cruis, 112 m.p.h.; hovering ceil. (out of ground effect), 4,760 ft.; service ceil., 13,120 ft.; range (with 1,984-lb. payload), 68 mls., (with auxiliary fuel), 444 mls.
Weight: Empty, 5,236 lb., max loaded, 7,715 lb.
Dimensions: Rotor diameter, 47 ft. 6¾ in.; fuselage length, 39 ft. 2 in.; overall height, 12 ft. 3½ in.
Notes: The Mi-2, is currently in large-scale production under licence in Poland by WSK Swidnik where it is being produced in four versions; a seven-passenger model, an agricultural model fitted with two external containers for a maximum of 1,984 lb. of dry chemicals, a freighter version with a 264-lb. capacity winch and the ability to carry 1,543 lb. internally or 1,764 lb. externally, and an ambulance with accommodation for four stretchers and one attendant. Initially flown in 1963, the Mi-2 has established two F.A.I.-recognised speed records for helicopters in its class, the latest, established on June 20, 1965, being 167·2 m.p.h. The Mi-2 was transferred to Poland after prototype development in the U.S.S.R.

MIL MI-6 (HOOK)

Country of Origin: U.S.S.R.

Type: Heavy transport helicopter.

Power Plants: Two Soloviev D-25V turboshafts each rated at 5,500 s.h.p.

Performance: Max. speed, 186 m.p.h.; normal cruise, 155 m.p.h.; range (with 13,228-lb. payload), 394 mls., (with 17,637-lb. payload), 385 mls., (with 26,455-lb. payload), 124 mls.; max. range, 652 mls.; service ceil., 14,764 ft.

Weights: Empty, 59,525 lb.; normal loaded, 89,287 lb.; maximum loaded, 93,696 lb.

Dimensions: Rotor diameter, 114 ft. 10 in.; fuselage length, 122 ft. 6 in.; overall height, 40 ft. 6 in.

Notes: First flown in 1957 and manufactured in some numbers since 1959, the Mi-6 was the world's largest helicopter until the début of the Mi-12, and serves in both civil and military forms, the latter having been delivered to the U.A.R., North Vietnam, and Indonesia. The civil version can accommodate 65 passengers, and as an ambulance 41 casualty stretchers may be carried. The military version can accommodate 70 fully-equipped paratroops. Auxiliary wings are fitted to off-load the main rotor in cruising flight, but these may be removed when the Mi-6 is operated as a flying crane or as a water-bomber for fire-fighting.

267

MIL MI-8 (HIP)

Country of Origin: U.S.S.R.

Type: General-purpose transport helicopter.

Power Plants: Two Izotov TB-2-117 turboshafts each rated at 1,500 s.h.p.

Performance: Max. speed, 155 m.p.h.; max. cruise, 143 m.p.g.; normal cruise, 125 m.p.h.; range (with 6,614-lb. payload), 248 mls., (with 8,818-lb. payload), 62 mls.; max. range, 280 mls., (with auxiliary fuel), 435 mls.; service ceil. (at 24,251 lb.), 13,120 ft.

Weights: Empty, 15,800 lb.; normal loaded, 24,251 lb.; maximum loaded, 26,455 lb.

Dimensions: Rotor diameter, 56 ft. 5 in.; fuselage length, 49 ft. 2½ in.; overall height, 14 ft. 9 in.

Notes: Evolved from the piston-engined Mi-4 but retaining few interchangeable components in its definitive production form, the Mi-8 is being manufactured in two commercial versions, one accommodating up to 28 passengers and the other being intended for the freight transportation role with a maximum cargo load of 8,818 lb. Either passenger or freight version may be converted for the ambulance role with 12 casualty stretchers and one medical attendant. A controllable winch and underside cargo hook for lifting slung loads up to 5,500 lb. may be fitted. The Mi-8 is replacing the Mi-4 in service with several air forces.

MIL MI-10K (HARKE)

Country of Origin: U.S.S.R.

Type: Heavy crane-type helicopter.

Power Plants: Two Soloviev D25V turboshafts each rated at 5,500 s.h.p.

Performance: (Specification is applicable to standard Mi-10 but, apart from range, is also generally applicable to the Mi-10K) Max. speed (with empty cargo platform), 124 m.p.h., (with high-density platform load weighing 26,455 lb.), 112 m.p.h.; range (with 26,455-lb. load), 155 mls.; max. range (with auxiliary fuel), 391 mls.; service ceil., 9,842 ft.

Weights: (Mi-10) Empty, 59,525 lb.; max. loaded, 95,790 lb.

Dimensions: Rotor diameter, 82 ft. 0 in.; overall length, 137 ft. 5 in.; overall height (Mi-10), 32 ft. 6 in.

Notes: The Mi-10K, which was entering production in 1969, is a derivative of the production Mi-10 (see 1966 edition) in which a supplementary cockpit with full controls is provided beneath the front fuselage, the height of the undercarriage has been reduced, and a maximum slung load is increased to 24,250 lb., this being further raised to 30,864 lb. with the installation of D25V turboshafts of 6,500 s.h.p. The Mi-10K is being manufactured for both civil and military roles.

269

MIL MI-12 (HOMER)

Country of Origin: U.S.S.R

Type: Heavy transport helicopter.

Power Plants: Four Soloviev D25 turboshafts each rated at 6,000 s.h.p. (6,500 s.h.p. available for emergency use).

Performance: Approx. max. speed, 180 m.p.h.; max. inclined climb (with 68,410-lb. payload), 590 ft./min.; max. ferry range, 3,100 mls.

Weights: Max. loaded, 198,000–202,000 lb.

Dimensions: (Approx.) Rotor diameter (each), 115 ft.; fuselage length, 131 ft. 3 in.

Notes: The Mi-12 is currently the world's largest helicopter, and the first prototype reportedly commenced its flight test programme in the autumn of 1968. The Mi-12 employs the dynamic components of the Mi-6 (see page 267), being in effect two Mi-6 power unit and rotor complexes mounted side-by-side at the tips of braced wings spanning some 240 ft. and married to a fuselage of entirely new design. On February 22, 1969 a prototype Mi-12 established new international records by lifting 68,409 lb. to an altitude of 9,678 ft., and August 6, 1969 the Mi-12 lifted 88,635 lb. to an altitude of 7,381 ft. The Mi-12 is probably primarily military but is claimed to accommodate 175–250 passengers in commercial form.

SIKORSKY HH-3E (S-61R)

Country of Origin: U.S.A.

Type: Medium rescue helicopter.

Power Plants: Two General Electric T58-GE-5 turbo-shafts each rated at 1,500 s.h.p.

Performance: Max. speed, 165 m.p.h.; max. cruise, 154 m.p.h.; max. inclined climb, 1,520 ft./min.; service ceil., 11,700 ft.; range (with external jettisonable fuel tanks), 748 mls.

Weights: Empty, 14,426 lb.; normal loaded, 19,500 lb.; max., 22,050 lb.

Dimensions: Rotor diameter, 62 ft. 0 in.; fuselage length, 56 ft. 7 in.; overall height, 18 ft. 1 in.

Notes: The HH-3E is an armoured rescue variant of the S-61R, and differs from the U.S.A.F.'s CH-3E support transport helicopter in having self-sealing fuel tanks, a retractable flight refuelling probe (permitting aerial refuelling from an HC-130P Hercules tanker), defensive armament and a rescue hoist. The HH-3F of the U.S. Coast Guard is similar but does not have armour, armament or self-sealing tanks. It features sophisticated electronic gear for automatic navigation, communications, and search and weather radar. The HH-3F can carry 20 passengers or nine casualty stretchers, and the CH-3E can accommodate up to 30 troops or 5,000 lb. of cargo.

SIKORSKY S-62 (HH-52A)

Country of Origin: U.S.A.

Type: Amphibious utility transport helicopter.

Power Plant: One General Electric CT58-110-1 (T58-GE-8) turboshaft rated at 1,250 s.h.p.

Performance: (HH-52A) Max. speed, 109 m.p.h.; max. cruise, 98 m.p.h.; max. inclined climb, 1,080 ft./min.; hovering ceil. (in ground effect), 12,200 ft., (out of ground effect), 1,700 ft.; range (with 10% reserves), 474 mls.

Weights: Empty equipped, 5,083 lb.; max. loaded, 8,100 lb.

Dimensions: Rotor diameter, 53 ft. 0 in.; fuselage length, 45 ft. 5½ in.; overall height, 16 ft. 0 in.

Notes: The S-62 embodies many components of the piston-engined S-55, including rotor blades, main and tail rotor heads, intermediate and tail gearboxes, and shafting. The basic model is the S-62A, a search and rescue version for the U.S. Coast Guard (described and illustrated above) being the HH-52A. Commercial and foreign military models essentially similar to the HH-52A are designated S-62C. Licence manufacture of the S-62A is undertaken in Japan by Mitsubishi primarily for the Air and Maritime Self-Defence Forces. Single examples of Mitsubishi-built S-62s have been supplied to Thailand and the Philippines.

272

SIKORSKY S-64 (CH-54 TARHE)

Country of Origin: U.S.A.

Type: Heavy flying crane helicopter.

Power Plants: Two Pratt & Whitney (CH-54A) JFTD12A-4A or (CH-54B) JFTD12A-5A turbo-shafts each rated at 4,500 s.h.p. and 4,800 s.h.p. respectively.

Performance: (CH-54B) Max. speed (without external load), 160 m.p.h.; max. cruise (at 47,000 lb.), 110 m.p.h. (CH-54A) max. speed (without external load), 125 m.p.h.; max. cruise (at 38,000 lb.), 109 m.p.h.; max. inclined climb, 1,700 ft./min.

Weights: Normal loaded (CH-54B), 47,000 lb. (CH-54A), 38,000 lb.; max. (CH-54B), 64,700 lb., (CH-54A) 42,000 lb.

Dimensions: Rotor diameter, 72 ft. 0 in.; fuselage length, (CH-54B) 80 ft. 7 in., (CH-54A) 70 ft. 3 in.; overall height, 25 ft. 5 in.

Notes: The CH-54A Tarhe entered service with the U.S. Army in 1965, and the improved CH-54B affording a 4,000-lb. increase in payload was first delivered to the U.S. Army in April 1969, 23 CH-54A helicopters currently being modified to CH-54B standards. A commercial version of the CH-54A, the S-64E (illustrated), entered service with Rowan Air Cranes in April 1969 for the support of oil operations.

SIKORSKY S-65A (CH-53)

Country of Origin: U.S.A.

Type: (CH-53) Heavy assault transport and (HH-53) combat aircrew rescue and recovery helicopter.

Power Plants: Two General Electric (HH-53C) T64-GE-7 or (CH-53D) T64-GE-400 turboshafts each rated at 3,435 s.h.p. and 3,925 s.h.p. respectively.

Performance: (HH-53C at 37,399 lb.) Max. speed, 186 m.p.h.; max. cruise, 172 m.p.h.; max. inclined climb 2,070 ft./min.; service ceil., 20,400 ft.

Weights: (HH-53C) Empty, 23,324 lb.; typical mission loaded, 37,399 lb.; max. loaded, 42,000 lb.

Dimensions: Rotor diameter, 72 ft. 2¾ in.; fuselage length, 67 ft. 2 in.; overall height, 22 ft. 0 in.

Notes: The CH-53A and -53D Sea Stallion are U.S. Marine Corps versions of the S-65A, the former having the 2,850 s.h.p. T64-GE-6. The first CH-53D was delivered to the U.S.M.C. on March 3, 1969, and Federal Germany is receiving 135 (illustrated) as the CH-53D/G. The Sea Stallion can accommodate 38 combat-equipped troops or 24 casualty stretchers. The HH-53B and -53C are rescue and recovery versions for the U.S.A.F., the former having 3,080 s.h.p. T64-GE-3s. The HH-53C is equipped for aerial re-fuelling, has jettisonable auxiliary fuel tanks, and is used by the Aerospace Rescue and Recovery Service.

SUD-AVIATION SA-319C ALOUETTE III

Country of Origin: France.
Type: Light utility helicopter.
Power Plant: One Turboméca Astazou XIV turbo-shaft rated at 922 s.h.p.
Performance: (At 4,960 lb.) Max. speed, 137 m.p.h.; max. cruise, 122 m.p.h.; max. inclined climb, 846 ft./min.; hovering ceil. (in ground effect), 5,740 ft.; range, 422 mls. at 6,560 ft.
Weights: Empty, 2,403 lb.; max. loaded, 4,960 lb.
Dimensions: Rotor diameter, 36 ft. 1 in.; fuselage length, 32 ft. 8¾ in.; overall height, 10 ft. 1½ in.
Notes: The Alouette III helicopter was initially flown on February 2, 1959, and has been in continuous production since 1961, a total of 734 having been ordered by the beginning of October 1969. The SA-319C is the latest derivative of the basic type, and although externally similar to the SE-3160 version (illustrated above) has an uprated Astazou XIV in place of the normal 870 s.h.p. Artouste IIIB, affording improved perform-ance under hot-and-high conditions and a 375-lb. increase in payload. The first prototype SA-319 (a conversion of the SE-3160 No. 001) was flown in 1967 with an Astazou XII, the definitive prototype flying on June 27, 1968, and production is expected to com-mence in 1970.

SUD-AVIATION SA-321 SUPER FRELON

Country of Origin: France.

Type: Medium transport and (SA-321G) anti-submarine warfare helicopter.

Power Plants: Three Turboméca Turmo IIIC.3 turboshafts each rated at 1,500 s.h.p.

Performance: Max. speed (at 24,250 lb.), 158 m.p.h. at sea level; max. cruise, 149 m.p.h.; max. inclined climb, 1,475 ft./min.; service ceil., 10,800 ft.; range (with 5,925-lb. payload), 234 mls.; ferry range 733 mls.

Weights: Empty, 14,640 lb.; normal loaded, 24,250 lb.; max. loaded, 26,455 lb.

Dimensions: Rotor diameter, 62 ft. 0 in.; fuselage length 62 ft. 3 in.; overall height, 16 ft. 2½ in.

Notes: Two prototypes and four pre-production examples of the SA-321 Super Frelon (Super Hornet) are currently being followed by 43 production examples, including 12 of the non-amphibious SA-321K transport version for the Israeli Defence Force and 16 similar SA-321Ls for the South African Air Force. The amphibious ASW version, the SA-321G, is being manufactured for France's *Aéronavale* as the SA-321Gb this having Sylph radars in the outrigger floats, dunking sonar, and up to four homing torpedoes and other ASW stores.

276

SUD-AVIATION SA-330 PUMA

Country of Origin: France.
Type: Tactical assault and transport Helicopter.
Power Plants: Two Turboméca Turmo IIIC.4 turbo-shafts each rated at 1,300 s.h.p.
Performance: Max. speed, 174 m.p.h. at sea level; normal cruise, 157 m.p.h.; max. inclined climb, 1,417 ft./min.; hovering ceil. (out of ground effect), 12,450 ft.; service ceil., 17,225 ft.; range (with 3,858-lb. payload), 230 mls.; ferry range, 905 mls. at 4,900 ft.
Weights: Empty, 7,253 lb.; normal loaded, 13,220 lb.; max. loaded, 14,110 lb.
Dimensions: Rotor diameter, 49 ft. 2½ in.; fuselage length, 46 ft. 1½ in.; overall height, 16 ft. 9¾ in.
Notes: The SA-330 has been developed specifically to a French Army requirement, and quantity production was initiated in 1967. The SA-330 has a crew of two and accommodates a maximum of 12 fully-equipped troops, and eight test and evaluation examples were built for the flight development programme, the first having flown on April 15, 1965. The first production SA-330 flew in September 1968, and plans currently call for the manufacture of 130 SA-330s for the French Army in collaboration with Westland, the British company assembling 40 for the R.A.F. Thirty-five Pumas have also been ordered by Portugal.

SUD-AVIATION SA-341 GAZELLE

Country of Origin: France.
Type: Light observation helicopter.
Power Plant: One Turboméca Astazou IIN.2 turbo-shaft rated at 600 s.h.p.
Performance: (At 3,530 lb.) Max. speed, 169 m.p.h. at sea level; econ. cruis., 137 m.p.h.; max. inclined climb, 1,650 ft./min.; hovering ceil. (in ground effect), 12,465 ft. (out of ground effect), 10,500 ft.; range, 426 mls.
Weights: Empty, 1,765 lb.; loaded, 3,530 lb.; max. overload, 3,750 lb.
Dimensions: Rotor diameter, 34 ft. 5½ in.; fuselage length, 30 ft. 10½ in; overall height, 9 ft. 8½ in.
Notes: The SA-341 is being manufactured under a joint Anglo-French programme as the standard light observation helicopter for both the British and French armed forces, the former having a requirement for some 600 and the latter approximately 100. The SA-341 is the production derivative of the SA-340, two prototypes of which have been tested, the first having flown on April 7, 1967, and the second, featuring the 13-blade shrouded anti-torque rotor to be utilised by the SA-341, flying on August 2, 1968. Four pre-production SA-341s have been built, and the first production helicopter is to fly mid-1970.

VFW-FOKKER VFW H3

Country of Origin: Federal Germany.

Type: Three-seat compound helicopter.

Power Plant: One Allison 250 turboshaft rated at 317 s.h.p.

Performance: (Estimated with 400 s.h.p. turboshaft) Max. speed, 155 m.p.h.; econ. cruise, 130 m.p.h.; max. inclined climb, 1,280 ft./min.; range, 310 mls.

Weights: Empty, 1,069 lb.; loaded, 2,127 lb.

Dimensions:: Rotor diameter, 28 ft. 6½ in.; fuselage length, 23 ft. 1½ in.; overall height, 8 ft. 2 in.

Notes: The H3 is a compound helicopter in which the turboshaft drives a centrifugal compressor supplying air to rotor tip nozzles, power being transferred to the ducted fans attached to the fuselage sides for cruising flight. The first of two prototypes was completed on October 6, 1968, and the initial test programme was initiated in 1969 with the H3 flying as a plain helicopter. These trials was scheduled to be followed by tests as a simple gyroplane, and subsequently as a combination of the two. The H3 will be able to perform jump-start take-offs with free-wheeling rotor, using a pre-take-off rotor spin-up technique. The H5 is a projected five-seat version.

279

WESTLAND SCOUT A.H. MK. 1

Country of Origin: United Kingdom.
Type: Light utility helicopter.
Power Plant: One Rolls-Royce Bristol Nimbus 102 turboshaft rated at 685 s.h.p.
Performance: Max. speed, 132 m.p.h.; max. cruise, 122 m.p.h.; max. inclined climb 1,670 ft./min.; hovering ceil. (in ground effect), 15,400 ft., (out of ground effect), 10,000 ft.; max. range (with standard fuel), 322 mls.
Weights: Empty, 3,184 lb.; max. loaded, 5,300 lb.
Dimensions: Rotor diameter, 32 ft. 3 in.; fuselage length, 30 ft. 7½ in.; overall height, 8 ft. 11 in.
Notes: Derived from the same basic design as the Wasp A.S. Mk. 1, the Scout is currently in production for and in service with the British Army, two have been supplied to the Royal Australian Navy, one to the Bahrein State Police, two to the Uganda Police Air Wing, and three to the Royal Jordanian Arab Army. For the ambulance role two casualty stretchers may be accommodated, and a sling for external freight and a power-operated rescue hoist may be fitted. The Scout may also carry wire-guided missiles such as the Nord SS.11, and up to five passengers may be carried. A number of components are similar to those of Wasp.
280

WESTLAND SEA KING H.A.S. MK. 1

Country of Origin: United Kingdom (U.S. licence).
Type: Amphibious anti-submarine warfare helicopter.
Power Plants: Two Rolls-Royce Bristol Gnome H.1400 turboshafts each rated at 1,500 s.h.p.
Performance: (At 20,500 lb.) Max. speed, 161 m.p.h.; normal cruise, 131 m.p.h.; max. inclined climb, 1,770 ft./min.; range (internal fuel), 690 mls.; max. ferry range (max. external fuel), 1,105 mls. at 5,000 ft.
Weights: Empty equipped, 15,474 lb.; max. loaded, 21,500 lb.
Dimensions: Rotor diameter, 62 ft. 0 in.; fuselage length, 54 ft. 9 in.; overall height, 15 ft. 11 in.
Notes: Westland is manufacturing 60 examples of an anglicised version of the Sikorsky SH-3D Sea King for the Royal Navy and 22 for the Federal German Navy, the first Westland-built example flying on May 7, 1969. Sea Kings are to be deployed at sea by the Royal Navy aboard carriers and converted *Tiger* class cruisers. In addition to the ASW role, the Sea King will perform mine countermeasures, air-to-surface strike, search-and-rescue, troop lift, casualty evacuation and cargo-carrying tasks in Royal Navy service. No. 700S Squadron was formed on the Sea King as a trials unit on August 19, 1969, and the first operational unit, No. 824 Sqdn., was formed in February 1970.

WESTLAND WASP A.S. MK. 1

Country of Origin: United Kingdom.
Type: Anti-submarine warfare helicopter.
Power Plant: One Rolls-Royce Bristol Nimbus 50 turboshaft rated at 710 s.h.p.
Performance: Max. speed, 121 m.p.h.; cruise, 110 m.p.h.; max. inclined climb, 1,440 ft./min.; hovering ceiling (in ground effect), 12,500 ft., (out of ground effect) 8,800 ft.; max. range, 303 mls.
Weights: Empty, 3,452 lb.; max. loaded, 5,500 lb.
Dimensions: Rotor diameter, 32 ft. 3 in., fuselage length 30 ft. 5¾ in., overall height, 9 ft. 9 in.
Notes: The Wasp A.S. Mk. 1 currently serves with the Royal Navy in the anti-submarine weapon-carrying role, operating from platforms aboard frigates equipped with long-range asdic. In this role the Wasp is normally crewed by a single pilot and carries two 270-lb. torpedoes. Dual controls may be fitted for the training role, and four passengers may be carried. The Wasp has been supplied to the Brazilian, Netherlands, New Zealand and South African navies. A specially designed undercarriage incorporating fully castoring lockable wheels permits normal operation aboard ship in heavy seas, and a power hoist, operated by the pilot or a crewman, is installed for rescue missions.

WESTLAND WESSEX H.U. MK. 5

Country of Origin: United Kingdom.
Type: Medium assault transport helicopter.
Power Plants: Two Rolls-Royce Bristol Gnome 110/111 turboshafts each rated at 1,350 s.h.p. (power limited to max. of 1,550 s.h.p. at rotor head).
Performance: (At 13,500 lb.) Max. speed, 132 m.p.h.; max. cruise, 121 m.p.h.; max. inclined climb, 1,650 ft./min.; hovering ceil. (out of ground effect), 4,000 ft.; range (max. fuel and 10% reserves), 478 mls.
Weights: Empty equipped, 8,657 lb.; max. loaded, 13,500 lb.
Dimensions: Rotor diameter, 56 ft. 0 in.; fuselage length, 48 ft. 4½ in.; overall height, 16 ft. 2 in.
Notes: The Wessex H.U. Mk. 5 commando assault helicopter of the Royal Navy is one of several anglicised, turbine-powered derivatives of the piston-engined Sikorsky S-58 which have been in continuous production in the U.K. since 1958. The H.A.S. Mks. 1 and 3 ASW versions for the Royal Navy are powered by single flat-rated Gazelle turboshafts, the coupled-Gnome installation having been introduced by the H.C. Mk. 2 utility transport version of the Wessex for the R.A.F. Export versions of the last-mentioned variant include the Mks. 52 (Iraq), 53 (Ghana), and 54 (Brunei).

283

WESTLAND WG.13

Country of Origin: United Kingdom.

Type: Medium utility and anti-submarine warfare helicopter.

Power Plants: Two Rolls-Royce Bristol 360-07 turbo-shafts each rated at 900 s.h.p.

Performance: (Estimated for utility version at 8,000 lb.) Max. speed, 184 m.p.h.; econ. cruise, 161 m.p.h.; max. inclined climb, 2,650 ft./min.; hovering ceiling (out of ground effect), 10,000 ft.; max. range (standard fuel, no reserves), 540 mls., (at 8,500 lb. with auxiliary fuel and reserves), 1,150 mls.

Weights: (Utility) Empty, 4,347 lb.; normal loaded 8,000 lb.

Dimensions: Rotor diameter, 42 ft. 0 in.; fuselage length, 38 ft. 3¼ in.; overall height, 12 ft. 0 in.

Notes: The WG.13 is one of the three types included in the Anglo-French helicopter programme, the others being the SA-330 Puma (see page 277) and SA-341 Gazelle (see page 278). A pre-production batch of five WG.13s has been ordered of which the first is scheduled to fly in December 1970. At the time of closing for press it was anticipated that the British Army will require 150 of the utility model, the R.N. and *Aéronavale* will respectively require 100 and 80 of the ASW version, and the R.A.F. will require 30 trainers.

INDEX OF AIRCRAFT TYPES

Made and Printed in Great Britain by
Butler & Tanner Ltd., Frome and London